Strangers and Neighbors

What I Have Learned About Christianity
from Living Among Orthodox Jews

Maria Poggi Johnson

www.wpublishinggroup.com

STRANGERS AND NEIGHBORS

Copyright © 2006 Maria Poggi Johnson

All rights reserved. No portion of this book may be reproduced, stored in a retrieval system, or transmitted in any form or by any means—electronic, mechanical, photocopy, recording, or any other—except for brief quotations in printed reviews, without the prior permission of the publisher.

Published by W Publishing Group, a division of Thomas Nelson, Inc., P.O. Box 141000, Nashville, Tennessee 37214.

W Publishing Group books may be purchased in bulk for educational, business, fund-raising, or sales promotional use. For information, please e-mail SpecialMarkets@ThomasNelson.com.

All Scripture quotations, unless otherwise indicated, are taken from the New Revised Standard Version Bible (NRSV), copyright © 1989 by the Division of Christian Education of the National Council of the Churches of Christ in the U.S.A. Used by permission. All rights reserved.

Editorial Staff: Kate Etue, acquisitions editor, Thom Chittom, managing editor
Cover Design: David Drummond
Page Design: Walter Petrie

Library of Congress Cataloging-in-Publication Data

Johnson, Maria Poggi.
    Strangers and neighbors / Maria Poggi Johnson.
     p. cm.
    ISBN-10: 0-8499-1151-6
    ISBN-13: 978-0-8499-1151-4
    1. Johnson, Maria Poggi. 2. Christian biography. 3. Christianity and other religions—Judaism. 4. Judaism—Relations—Christianity. I. Title.
    BR1725.J622A3 2006
261.2'6092—dc22
                                       2006005932

Printed in the United States of America

06 07 08 09 10 RRD 5 4 3 2 1

BIO
JOHNSON,
M.

Contents

Preface   v

1. And Was Jerusalem Builded Here?   1

2. People of the Book   11

3. Kosher Cake   23

4. The Holy God and His Stiff-Necked People   35

5. Good Shabbos   49

6. Why Is this Night Unlike All Other Nights?   59

7. Train Up a Child in the Way He Should Go   71

8. Not a Jot nor a Tittle   85

9. Darkness and the Triumph of Light   97

10. God Shows No Partiality   111

11. Us and Them   121

12. One Is Hashem   133

    Glossary   145

    Notes   151

    About the Author   152

iii

Preface

The subject of this book is not Judaism, nor Orthodox Judaism in contemporary America, nor even the particular brand of Orthodox Judaism practiced in my neighborhood. These are books I would like to read but am unqualified to write. The subject of this book is my own experience, and that of my family, living as Catholic Christians in proximity to a community of strictly observant Orthodox Jews and in friendship with a handful of families in that community. The only point of view I represent with any consistency is my own. Names of individuals have been changed. (Thanks for the list of names, Menucha!)

A minimum of background may be useful. We live in a small city in northeastern Pennsylvania—a former mining community—where there is a community of some sixty or seventy families of Orthodox Jews, mostly clustered in the Hill Section where we live. The Jews in our neighborhood are from the stricter end of the Orthodox spectrum: what are popularly called "ultra-Orthodox" or "black hatters." (For the most part, they do not belong to the various Hasidic groups, although there are a number of Lubavitcher families.)

There is a saying: "Two Jews, three opinions." Judaism is a very diverse and wonderfully argumentative tradition. So when I say "Jews do *x*" or "Jews believe *y*," I do so for the sake of brevity. The opinions I cite here are those of the person who happened to be nearest when I thought of the question. Maybe if I had turned to the person on my left instead of to the person on my right, I would have come away with quite a different picture. Although the kind of Judaism represented by my friends and neighbors is the fastest-growing form in the world today, the considerable majority of American Jews do not live at all like my neighbors. My neighbors, by and large, would say that their form of observance is the authentic one and that all Jews *should* live like them. Most Jews from the Reform and Conservative traditions, and even from the more liberal end of Orthodoxy, would disagree.

But these are questions internal to Judaism, and it is no business of mine to have opinions on what Jews should or should not believe or do, or how Judaism ought to be practiced. My business is simply to communicate some of what I have learned from living here, in daily contact with a vibrant Jewish life and in conversation and friendship with individuals and families. I have done my best to represent what people have told me as accurately as possible and to make clear the distinction between their perspectives and my own. Any errors are due to my own, inadvertent, misunderstanding. Of course, my understanding of Judaism is that of a Christian and thus is very different from theirs. In particular, my interpretations of Scripture are entirely my own and are often quite different from traditional Jewish understandings of the same passages.

I have many people to thank. For practical support, I am indebted to my colleagues at the University of Scranton: in particular, Joe Dreisbach, Brigid Frein, Charlie Pinches, Marc Shapiro, and Marie Gaughan. Damon Linker at *First Things* published a short essay I wrote on this subject. Kate Etue approached me with the idea for this book and has been most generous with guidance, understanding, and encouragement from the beginning. Thom Chittom steered me through the final stages of the process. Crystal Lee gave me many tranquil child-free hours to write. Sarah Farrimond, Bill Maughan, Barbara Gaynor, and Detra Damskov have kindly read and commented on sections.

My principle debt, of course, is to our Jewish friends and neighbors. Many people, including some whose names I don't know, have been kind and helped to put me at ease in situations in which it would be easy for a Gentile to feel very much out of place. I need to thank in particular, for their hospitality and patience with my interminable and often muddle-headed questions, Mazal Minkoff, Devorah Leah Selincourt, the Weinreb and Davidson families, and most especially Shanie Davidson, for friendship and guidance.

Many people have educated me, encouraged me, listened

to me, advised me, and supported me. My husband, Glen Johnson, has done all of this and much, much more. He has done most of the laundry, the cooking, the shopping, and the diapers for months on end and never once complained. He has also read everything in this book about a dozen times, and although he will never admit to it, he must be heartily sick of it by now. Nonetheless, it is dedicated to him with much love.

❧ 1 ❧

And Was Jerusalem Builded Here?

One evening at sundown, several years ago now, I stood transfixed and watched as the Sabbath came and was greeted by her own as a queen.

I was on a study tour with a group of colleagues: professors from the theology department of the Jesuit university where I teach. Our wonderfully well-funded Judaic Studies program had offered to send us to Israel for ten days, and my husband, blessed be he, had more or less pushed me onto the plane, insisting that, of course, he could manage the baby (our first, weaned just in time) perfectly well by himself and that I couldn't miss this chance and that he'd get to go some other time, not to worry, and would you just leave, already? So there I was. We had spent the previous five days in the north, looking out from Mount Carmel where Elijah faced down the prophets of Baal, visiting Jesus's synagogue at Capernaeum, hearing Mass on the beach where he fed five thousand hungry souls with a few loaves and fishes—and it had all been thrilling.

That day—Friday—we got up before the sun to leave Galilee and head south. We had to be on the road indecently early to be sure we would make it to Jerusalem by sundown; my colleague Marc is an observant Orthodox Jew and can't be in a car after sundown on Friday, when the Sabbath begins. So we yawned our way through a bleary pre-dawn breakfast and hit the road. We drove through the lovely and intimidating Judaean desert, where the rocks, uncomplicated by vegetation, are bleached and polished by the sun in a thousand delicate shades. We stopped for lunch at an all-you-can-eat buffet overlooking the Mount of the Temptation (I promise, there really is one), trekked down a blazing gully to a fifteen-hundred-year-old monastery set into the side of a cliff, and arrived, dusty and tired, at a Sheraton in a Jerusalem suburb.

The more sensible ones among us showered, ate dinner, and went to their rooms to write in their journals and rest; but four of us, each drawn by the same impulse, threw our bags down and met back in the lobby five minutes later. We were in Jerusalem—*Jerusalem!*—and as tired as we were, the thought of hanging around in hotel rooms that might well have been in New Jersey was intolerable.

The sun was nearing the horizon. We jumped in a taxi, which took us to one of the gates of the ancient walled city. Marc couldn't touch money for the next twenty-four hours, so he hung back while we paid the driver, and then he led us to the Wall. The Wall is the western face of the Temple Mount. It is all that is left of the Temple and the only physical remainder of the days when Jews were safe in their own land, masters of the entire region. It is often called the Wailing Wall—faithful Jews, battered by the horrors of the past and the bitterness of the present, go there to mourn the destruction of the Temple and the passing of the days when the Ark of the Covenant was in the Holy of Holies and the name of the God of Israel was revered everywhere. The Wall is ancient; it has absorbed history, soaking it in through its pores, and it exudes the ancient, sacred, lost past into the air of the modern square with its metal detectors and lounging teenage soldiers.

I am usually one to be impressed by old things, but this evening the present was intensely more interesting than the past. The mood among the Jews who crowded the plaza to welcome the Sabbath was one not of lamentation, nostalgia, loss, or bitterness, but of joy: deep and serious and exultant joy. Mature men with full beards and long black coats, men exuding gravitas as the Wall exuded antiquity, were dancing and singing with abandon. It was alien and intense and thrilling.

And it was important.

I'm a scholar, trained to keep a rein on my personal responses and to regard everything from a safe, analytical distance, but there was no question of my coolly observing the scene as an interesting cultural-religious phenomenon. I found myself quite certain that something really was happening as the sun slipped behind the rooftops of Jerusalem; that the whirling, singing crowds were responding to a reality greater than any culture. It mattered, deeply, that they were there, spinning and rejoicing and praying and welcoming *Shabbos Malka*, the Queen of Sabbath.

From that moment, although we saw all kinds of things—the Church of the Nativity in Bethlehem, the garden of Gethsemane, the Via Dolorosa, the Church of the Holy Sepulcher—that put flesh and rock and color on the stories of the Bible, I was more interested in the present. I kept coming back to the Wall. Whenever we had a minute free, I'd go there and watch the people who came to pray: not the hordes of tourists who would shuffle to the front for a minute and turn back again, but the strange people in strange clothes who stood for hours in the sun rocking back and forth over open books. (I was particularly intrigued by the Satmar, a Hasidic group who wear black satin dressing gowns with huge cylindrical fur hats.) I pored over the religious posters and polemical flyers that were all across Jerusalem, and I interrogated Marc relentlessly about the varieties of Orthodoxy. My colleagues, knowing my story—my thoroughly secular childhood, my adolescent conversion, my wanderings through various corners of Christianity, my recent coming to rest in the Roman Catholic Church—pretended to worry that I might convert yet again. Once, we came out of a café and ran into a bizarre group of Americans, who had taken over the square and were dancing, waving flags, handing out leaflets, whooping, "Yeshua is Lord! Alleluia!" and talking with near-hysterical enthusiasm to anyone would listen. As far as I could make out, I think they were Judaizers: twentieth-century descendants of the people whom Paul scolded the Galatians for following. (They were Gentile Christians who considered themselves to have converted to Judaism while remaining Christian, or some such.) But I never did quite figure out exactly what their thing was, because the others hauled me off: "Get Maria out of here, and quick! What are we going to tell Glen if she runs off with them?"

I wasn't, of course, about to run off and start handing out pamphlets about Yeshua haMoshiach. And perhaps I should say right now that the thought of converting to Judaism has never crossed my mind for a second, ever. In fact, one of the things that fascinated me about the Orthodox was that, while they were passionately, even outlandishly, religious, they had no desire to convince me to be like them. I'd spent plenty of time around people whose Christianity, as far as I could tell, consisted almost exclusively of trying to persuade (and sometimes manipulate or bully) other people to be Christians. In fact, I'd been one of them myself, and my motives had been complex and mixed and had made me very uncomfortable. The Orthodox who prayed at the Wall were certain—so much so that their certainty infected me—that it was crucial, not just to them but to all of creation, that they be there. But it was *their* job, given to them by God, and they did not ask me to share it.

My fascination with the compelling strangeness of the Orthodox Judaism I saw at the Wall was all the greater because it was not entirely new to me. A year before the Israel trip, my husband and I had moved into a beautiful but dilapidated Victorian house five blocks from campus. Buying it had been a piece of romantic folly. It had gorgeous pocket doors, a lovely tiled fireplace, stained glass windows, and even a turret; but it also had a crumbling staircase, splintered siding, caved-in ceilings, and lethally archaic wiring, which was why we could afford it. The neighborhood was a bit iffy, but the house was two blocks from one Orthodox synagogue, four blocks from another, and three from the Hebrew Day School that served a healthy and growing Orthodox community. We told ourselves that it surely had to be a safe place to live, signed the contract, and got to work.

So when I came home to Glen and the baby, it was to a neighborhood with a very visible Jewish life. I wanted to walk up to people in the street and say, "Hello! I just got back from Jerusalem!" in the hope that they would talk to me about it and make me feel connected to a place I missed after being there only five days, but I was restrained by my reluctance to make a complete idiot of myself in front of strangers. My pregnancy had put me on nodding terms with many of the women on my route to work, and I had even ventured a tentative "Good Shabbos" on Saturdays, but I still regarded our Jewish neighbors with a combination of bewilderment, awe, and intense curiosity. If I was on my way home when the Day School was letting out or when the men were leaving the shul (synagogue) after prayers, I would walk slowly—it's embarrassing to admit it—in hopes of overhearing bits of their conversations. I assumed that such serious people would talk only about weighty matters: I thought I would hear sentences beginning, "When our forefather Abraham sat under the terebinth at Mamre . . ." Of course, when I was successful in my eavesdropping, I invariably heard about the weather forecast or the rudeness of the pediatrician's receptionist or the clearance at Sears—precisely what Catholics and Baptists, and presumably everybody else talk about when they are hanging around the school doors waiting for their kids.

That was eight years ago, and the house is very different now. Glen has wired and plumbed and insulated and plastered, knocked down walls and put up walls, rebuilt the stairs, refinished floors, built bookcases, and painted. This is how it works for academic couples: unless one of you is such a star that you can write your own ticket and your spouse's to boot (we aren't), or unless you get outrageously lucky and get jobs in the same place (we didn't), or unless you are prepared to have a commuter marriage (we weren't), you go to wherever the first person gets a job and the other one picks up part-time teaching or translates ancient Greek treatises or changes diapers or restores Victorian houses or somehow manages to do them all at once.

The house is a good deal fuller too. We have had four

children in six years, bringing the total of children on the block to about forty—most of them Orthodox Jews. We are on weather-forecast and pediatrician's-receptionist terms with all of the Orthodox families on our block, and two of them have become our good friends. The women and I lend each other maternity clothes and go to the gym together; our husbands borrow each other's snow shovels and power tools and grumble about local politics; our children are in and out of each other's houses most days. Ours have picked up a smattering of Hebrew: "You have to share, it's a mitzvah," my little Catholic daughters tell each other. And they occasionally make vain attempts to reject undesirable foodstuffs on the grounds, "I don't think celery is kosher." Our initiation into home ownership and neighborhood life has been rather odd but could not have been better.

Now, of course, one doesn't have to be an Orthodox Jew to be a good neighbor or desirable playmate. Most likely we just happened to land among particularly nice, friendly people who would have been every bit as nice and friendly had they been Episcopalians or Hindus or Elvis-worshipers or atheists. But living in daily contact with a vital and vibrant Jewish life has been fascinating and transforming for my family as Christians.

Before we came here, we knew, as all Christians know, that Christianity is rooted deeply in Judaism. And as my husband and I are trained theologians, we probably had a rather clearer sense than most Christians of exactly what that involves. But while we were able to chart the web of typological connections between the Testaments or explain the relevance of the Jewish sacrificial system to an understanding of the Crucifixion, we had no real sense of Judaism as a living reality.

It has been six years since I watched in puzzled awe as the Sabbath Queen was welcomed into the plaza by the Western Wall, and since then I have stood with a baby on my hip while she was welcomed into the living room of our neighbors four doors down. I have been to a bris, to a bar mitzvah, and to parties for Hanukkah and Sukkot. Of course, I'm well over my initial silly awe and shyness, but the sense of mystery and significance that held me spellbound at the Wall has not been eroded by ease and familiarity. When I watch the Shabbos candles being lit or stand on the women's side of the shul while men in striped prayer shawls cluster around a wailing infant, I feel sure that what is going on is of profound importance—and not just subjectively, to the people around me, but objectively, to me and to the world.

I am, and will remain, a Christian; but I am a rather different Christian now than I was before.

2

People of the Book

A few weeks ago, Ahuva called me from her cell phone. There was a lot of noise in the background: "They're finishing a new Torah scroll for the shul," she said. "Did you see it in the paper? They're in the Jewish Home now writing the last few words. They'll be leaving in a few minutes and dancing it across the street. The kids are all here—you guys want to come see?"

I had indeed seen the story in the paper a few days earlier. Torah scrolls are hand-lettered by highly trained scribes, beautifully decorated, and encased in rich covers. The completion of one is a big event, and this was likely a once-in-a-lifetime opportunity for us. It was a nice day, so we called the kids, hunted around for sandals, scooped the baby into the stroller, and set off walking. When we arrived we found a police car blocking the street and a policeman surrounded by boys in yarmulkes and tzitzis squabbling over whose turn it was to hold the handcuffs next. Cathrine and Elisabeth spotted Yaffa, Dovid, Nechama, and Moshe and raced off to join them. We pushed the stroller round to the door and found Ahuva and Chana in the crowd of women and little children hanging around waiting for the action.

After a few minutes the back door opened, letting out first a confused rush of sound and then, in slow waves, a crush of men and boys in black suits and broad hats singing, jumping, and jostling around a swaying fringed canopy, under which Rabbi Rubin, our neighbor from three doors down, was clutching the scroll in its case. I felt the thrill of the timeless and immediate mystery that had captivated me in Jerusalem years before—until a young man in a yarmulke and baggy jeans began accompanying the singing with a battered-looking synthesizer, which rather took the edge off the atmosphere. It was, I suppose, an odd scene to come across in a neighborhood first established by WASP managers and accountants from the anthracite mines, but none of it strikes me as odd anymore. The only anomaly that day was me, in jeans with my hair uncovered.

It took about twenty minutes for the scroll to travel the two hundred yards from the home to the shul, advancing by fits and starts in the midst of an exuberant, swaying, bouncing, singing crowd. As they passed us, Ahuva— long acquainted with my intense curiosity about all things Orthodox—told me that the canopy carried over the Torah was the chuppah under which Jewish marriages take place, because, she said, "It's the Torah that marries us to God."

Oddly enough, it is in part my contact with Judaism that has, if not married me to the Bible, at least helped to heal what had for some time been a troubled relationship. It's a long story and is best cut short. I was raised in an entirely secular home and came to faith as a teenager, attracted by the warm, bright life of a group of Christians I stumbled across on the winding road through adolescence. I learned from them, and from the Christians who formed much of my social world most of the way through college, to read the Bible as a treatise in systematic theology: a series of closely interlocking propositions. Scripture was often disguised, for reasons that were never clear to me, as history, poetry, legal codes, and the like, but it was really a collection of theological statements to be discovered and believed. In the literature I studied and loved in college, truth presented itself in rich and varied forms, but when it came to the Bible, I had learned, the only kind of truth worth its salt was literal truth. To suggest that the Bible "worked" in some other way was tantamount to claiming that it was not the Word of God after all.

I did my best, but I could never manage to see in the Bible what my friends told me I should see. I always felt bullied by it. As much as I loved and respected the people whose friendship brought me first and always to God, I was frustrated that, while we talked and talked and talked endlessly and passionately about doctrine and truth and interpretation and Scripture, we never seemed to talk much about God himself. And it was God I was really curious about.

My graduate studies in church history and hermeneutics convinced me that the way I had been trying and failing to understand the Bible just wasn't going to work. But I didn't know any other way to read it, and at the time (what with falling in love, writing a dissertation, and looking for a job), I had enough on my plate without trying to figure out what I was supposed to do with the Bible too. The whole thing made me anxious and unhappy, and the simplest expedient seemed to be just to stop reading it altogether. For several years I did just that.

I got married, finished my dissertation, and stepped into the notoriously bleak academic job market. My grad school mentors, who groomed me for the ritualized torture of interviews and who were well aware of my British tendency to self-deprecation, told me over and over, "When they ask you whether you can teach such and such a course, the correct answer is *yes*. You understand, Maria? Say *yes*. If you get the job, you can worry about it then."

I did as I was told and, to my amazement, got the first job I interviewed for: at a Jesuit university with a downtown campus three blocks from where, now, the scroll was slowly progressing across the street. In my first semester the department chair assigned me to teach a freshman class on the Bible. Well, why wouldn't he? Hadn't I said, in my interview, "Sure, I could teach 'Introduction to the Bible.' No problem"? Obedient to my mentors' instructions, I had omitted to mention that I regarded the Bible with a mixture of suspicion and guilt, had barely picked it up in several years, and had never, at all, even a little bit, studied it as an academic subject. It was, all in all, a rather wobbly foundation on which to construct a college syllabus, but that is what I had to do.

I buckled down, read a lot of books, asked a lot of questions, and got a dizzying but invigorating amount of advice. The bit I liked best came from a colleague who said simply, "I try to get the students to see it as an unfolding narrative." This appealed to me because I like narratives, stories. I like them a great deal. Most of my youth (I never really learned to talk to people my own age until I got to college) had been spent devouring huge Victorian novels at a rate of about a thousand pages a week. I thought if I could approach the Bible as another big novel, I might get on with it better than I had previously. So I took courage and put together a syllabus on the sophisticated scholarly principle of starting at the beginning, going on from there, and seeing what happened.

On the day of my first class, feeling rather ill with nerves and very self-conscious in proper grown-up clothes (for me, anything that isn't jeans), I walked past the shul, past the Hebrew Day School, past the library, into St. Thomas Hall and, before going to my new office, stopped in at the little chapel in the basement. I knelt by the tabernacle where the candle was burning and, for about the thousandth time that summer, thanked God for bringing me there and giving me the opportunity to teach. I said the sort of things I thought I should about giving my work over to God for his glory, but I didn't really know what I meant by it. Before I left I said what was really on my mind: "Look, if I do this all wrong, if I teach nonsense or falsehood, please don't let it mess my students up. Just make them forget anything I say that won't be good for them."

What my students would have thought that semester if they knew that ten minutes before the start of every class their theology professor was on her knees asking God to make them forget everything she taught them, I don't know. Nor, for that matter, do I know to what extent God found it necessary to take me at my word and routinely erase my students' memories as soon as they were out of my clutches. But that daily prayer, as perverse and neurotic as it may seem, did at least help to erase many of my anxieties. I more or less grabbed my students by the hand and plunged into the text with them, and to my delight I found it both exhilarating and peaceful to let myself be washed around by the great rolling waves of salvation history. The students didn't seem to mind how many times I answered their questions with a cheerful, "Hmm, you know, I really can't tell you. I'll look it up. In the meantime let's go on and see what happens next."

What happened at first was that a people came, through a series of extraordinary experiences, to understand themselves to be chosen: set apart, claimed in a unique way by a God who was unlike all other gods, and who made extraordinary demands of them. They rejoiced in this, and they fought against it. They built a society worthy of their high calling, and they fell into the basest of sins. They loved and praised God in words and acts of timeless beauty, and they defied and neglected him in acts of rebellion and indifference. They made manifest to the nations the holiness of the Most High, and they broke his heart. They destroyed themselves, and they rediscovered themselves and their God in the midst of their destruction. It was a very good story indeed.

I was having so much fun with the story that I might very easily have stayed there and simply made my peace with the Bible as "great literature." Certainly there's more than enough in the Bible to keep the lover of great literature busy and happy for a lifetime. But on my way to class, that first seat-of-my-pants year, I walked past groups of men in black hats emerging from the shul, and past the Hebrew Day School where raucous Hebrew songs were spilling out of the windows and little boys in skullcaps were playing baseball in the yard. My students and I would read about God calling Abraham, about Jacob wrestling with God, about the people of Israel walking through the midst of the Red Sea, about Moses coming down from Mount Sinai bearing the tablets of the Law, about David repenting brokenhearted before God, about Solomon dedicating the Temple, about Isaiah pleading with the people to turn and be healed, about angels telling terrified shepherds that a king was born in Israel, about Jesus in the Temple telling his mother, "Didn't you know I'd be in my Father's house?" And then I would walk home and the Day School would be letting out and women in long skirts, their hair hidden under snoods, would be calling, "Tzipporah, over here, honey," or "Put that *down*, Yosef!"

The surprise and the strangeness of it—of living down the road from descendants of Abraham and Isaac and Jacob, from blood relatives of Moses, Aaron, and David, of Hosea, Hezekiah, and Nehemiah, of Mary, Caiaphas, Peter, and Paul—jolted me out of my Bible-as-great-literature phase before I'd really had time to settle in and kept me from taking a Jesus-as-great-moral-teacher approach to the New Testament. The story, very obviously, was alive and well. You don't run into the descendants of Oliver Twist or find yourself living down the road from people who trace their ancestry back to Anna Karenina or Huck Finn. The Bible was a wonderful story, great literature to be sure, but it was a lot more besides. When I asked God to protect my students from my mistakes, it seems I might have been the one most in need of help, and he used my Jewish neighbors to help me.

So there we were, following those neighbors as the scrolls were danced into the shul (Glen reached into his pocket for the yarmulke he keeps for such occasions) and were put into their place in the *Aron Kodesh* at the front. By this time the baby was getting squirmy and hungry, so we made sure the other kids were in the keeping of people who would get them home safely, and we walked home, leaving the scroll still surrounded by a surging, singing crowd. It will be taken out and read on Mondays and Thursdays and Saturdays. On the other days of the week, at all hours, the study rooms in the shul will house men, young and old, in pairs or groups, "sitting and learning" as the phrase goes: studying heavy, leather-bound Hebrew books. Studying Torah (although, strictly speaking, the Torah is the five books of Moses, the word is often used more generally to refer to the whole of Jewish law and life) is central to Orthodox life: an activity worth doing entirely for its own sake, and one that benefits all Jews everywhere.

Ironically, while our Jewish neighbors gave me back the Bible as a living book, they would disapprove thoroughly of the way I read it. I have made my peace, for the most part, with the historical and critical scholarship I was taught in my youth to regard as the primrose path to infidelity. I am quite comfortable, for instance, with the idea that the Pentateuch—the Torah, the five books of Moses— is a patchwork of different sources that probably didn't reach its final form until Moses had been dead for hundreds of years. I have no problem with the idea that the Ten Commandments reflect the Sinai experience, while the covenant code, in the chapters that follow, grow out of Israel's attempt to understand God's will in the details of daily life in the Promised Land. This perspective on the Bible makes sense of all sorts of things that don't make sense to me otherwise, and it solves all sorts of perplexing problems. However, my Orthodox neighbors would agree with my first Christian friends that this approach is a dangerous and irreverent compromise with secularism. The books of Moses, they say, are precisely what they claim to be: books written by Moses and passed on in their original form. The instructions about property damage by livestock, for instance, or about the proper procedure for preventing the spread of infectious diseases, were given by God to Moses. That's what happened; some unknown redactor from the era of David and Solomon didn't just decide that was the best way to organize the material.

On this, we disagree. We agree, however, on another point that I think is more important. We agree that the Bible must be read in company—that, regardless of exactly how it was written, if we are to receive the Bible as the Word of God, we must read it not as individuals but as members of a community.

According to Jewish tradition, Moses received from God not just the five books of the Torah but also a mass of other material expanding on and explaining the stories and laws in the Torah. This material was passed down for centuries by word of mouth—hence its name, the Oral Torah—until it was put down in writing somewhere between two hundred and five hundred years after the destruction of the Temple. These writings, called the Talmud, are the essential companion to the proper study of Torah and are, in their turn, the object of a vast and lively tradition of rabbinic commentary that is still alive. When Jews read Genesis, for example, they do so in the company of the Talmud, of centuries of rabbis, and of their friends, hunched over dining room tables or desks in the study rooms of shuls.

I think this is the way to do it. There are times when I read the Bible alone, but for the most part I do it with others. My partners are different from theirs: the fathers of the first Christian centuries (Irenaeus, Origen, Athanasius, Augustine), the ecclesiastics who put together the lectionary of the Catholic Church and decided which readings from the Old Testament ought to go side by side with ones from the Epistles and the Gospels, scholars in the historical-critical tradition, the evangelicals who brought me to faith, my husband, my fellow parishioners, my pastor, my colleagues, my students, and, now, my Jewish friends. Each of these partners has shed light on different aspects of the text and has raised different questions or pointed to different sets of possibilities. (I've made occasional brief attempts to read the Bible in company with the Talmud, but very quickly realized why devout Jews spend their whole lives learning it; it's quite impenetrably dense and difficult, really not the sort of stuff you can figure out without years of practice.)

Jesus says, "Do not think that I have come to abolish the law or the prophets; I have come not to abolish but to fulfill. For truly I tell you, until heaven and earth pass away, not one letter, not one stroke of a letter, [not 'one jot or one tittle' says the King James version, rather more memorably] will pass from the law until all is accomplished" (Matt. 5:17–18).

Christians believe that in Christ we have the true key to understanding the spirit of the Torah: that the Old Testament is fulfilled in the New. But while we believe that the fulfillment, the ending of the story, has been revealed, we are very obviously not there yet. Jews and Christians are both still waiting. Every letter, every stroke of every letter, every jot and tittle in the new scroll that lives in the Aron Kodesh down the road from us, is lovingly transcribed and preserved. And every nuance, every possible interpretation of every stroke, is pored over by a great cloud of witnesses: by the sages of the Talmud, by the great medieval scholars Maimonides and Nachmanides, and by our neighbors— Dr. Schwartz from across the road, Zevi from four doors down, and Mr. Cohen from the next block. They will not stop doing so until every stroke of every letter is fulfilled in plain sight of all.

3

Kosher Cake

It is the day before our son's second birthday, and his sisters, sensing that the grown-ups do not have the situation fully in hand, have decided that it is up to them to make him a cake. They have assembled quantities of mixing bowls, wooden spoons, oven gloves, rolling pins, and cookbooks in the middle of the kitchen floor and only need one thing from me before getting to work: "It has to be a kosher cake," they tell me, "so that Yaffa-Dovid-Ester can come over and have a party. Where is the kosher food to make it with?"

It's not going to happen. There is nothing, but nothing, that we can make for our Jewish neighbors to eat. As practiced by the Orthodox, the Jewish food laws of kashruth are not just a matter of avoiding bacon cheeseburgers. Meat has to come from certain animals, which have to be slaughtered in a very particular way, and the meat then rinsed and salted and rinsed again to remove all the blood, all under proper supervision.

The most complicated cluster of regulations comes from Exodus 23:19b, "You shall not boil a kid in its mother's milk." The original purpose of the prohibition is obscure, but through centuries of Jewish life and experience and reflection, it has developed into an absolute prohibition of the mixing of meat and dairy. As practiced by my neighbors, this involves two sets of plates and knives and forks and pots and pans (three in some households— actually twice as many—because come Pesach everything in the kitchen has to be boxed up and put away). Milk dishes and meat dishes have to be kept in separate cupboards, washed with different sponges in different sinks, and, for the very strictest families, cooked in separate ovens. Everything in our kitchen is hopelessly contaminated, and short of inviting a rabbi in with a blowtorch to *kasher* my entire kitchen, there's not a thing I can do about it.

There are different schools of thought on the positive function of the food laws. There are scholars who say the laws originated as hygienic measures: that pork was forbidden because it goes bad quickly in hot climates. Whether or not there's anything to that theory, it's not very interesting, and in any case it doesn't explain why people with refrigerators keep kosher today. I have friends, at the liberal end of Reform Judaism, who keep their homes kosher by choice, because they feel a responsibility to maintain the tradition and culture that have been made sacred by millennia of devotion and by millions of devoted lives. A colleague at the liberal end of Orthodoxy tells me the purpose of the laws is to provide an occasion for obedience. Ideally, he says, if a Jew sees someone eating bacon or lobster, he should think, *That looks really good. But the Torah forbids me to eat it, so I won't because I am a Jew.* (He freely admits that if you've grown up kosher, the idea of eating pigs or crustaceans is just gross, but the principle holds nonetheless.)

If you look at it this way, keeping kosher is a spiritual discipline of roughly the same sort as the Lenten fast in Catholic tradition. During Lent, every time I think, *Oh, what I wouldn't give for a cup of tea,* or a donut, or a glass of wine, or a lazy evening in front of the TV, or whatever it is that I have taken on as my fast that year, I am reminded that I don't because the Son of God emptied himself for me, poured himself out, hungered and thirsted and suffered and died for me. And here I am feeling sorry for myself because I've got a no-caffeine headache, which is my own stupid fault for getting addicted to the stuff in the first place and in any case hardly stacks up against crucifixion. Or for that matter against what millions of my fellow creatures go through every day. I really need to get over myself! If I go through this thought process five or six times a day for six weeks in the year, maybe I *will* get over myself, just a very little, and draw a little nearer to God, who has drawn near to me.

So, by my colleague's account, keeping kosher is like a really serious year-round fast, demanding sustained attention and care and focus and a continual reaffirmation of

what God has done and what it means for his people. But
he is what is called "Modern Orthodox"; my Jewish neighbors are, well, not-Modern Orthodox. Their understanding of what is going on is rather different. "Food doesn't
just feed the body; it feeds the soul too," Chana tells me.
(Chana is a *baal teshuvah*, a returnee: Jewish by birth
but raised in a secular household, she found her way to
Orthodoxy as an adult. She will admit to occasional culi-
nary nostalgia: "I used to eat a *lot* of seafood!") In her
view, certain foods or combinations of foods are declared
impure and forbidden, not as pretext for a bit of spiritual
discipline, but because they *are* impure. If you eat them,
the impurity will enter your soul, and your understanding
of and love for Torah will be muddied. So you make very
sure that your kitchen and everything you put in your
mouth meet God's standards.

This is one of the areas in which I find it almost
impossible to communicate with my neighbors, because
we are working with fundamentally different sets of con-
cepts. "What if you took every precaution," I have asked
them, "bought and cooked your food carefully, but despite
all your sincere efforts were deceived or tricked into eating
something nonkosher? Would it matter?"

What I want to know is whether the problem lies in the
food itself or in the attitude of mind—deliberate defiance
or mere carelessness—that would result in a Jew eating
something forbidden. *Does* what you don't know hurt you?
I have the hardest time getting an answer to this because, I

think, the question grows out of notions that are specific to Christian moral theology—in particular the idea, voiced by Jesus in Matthew's Sermon on the Mount, that what is in our hearts defines us more completely than our outward actions. This distinction is so much part of the way I think that I assume everybody must see things the same way. But it does not seem to be part of the way my neighbors see the world. They do their best to figure out what I am on about and give me an answer, but it is obvious that the question sounds arbitrary and pointless and we always run into a dead end.

This in itself is telling. One of the things that Christianity learns from Judaism (besides, oh, let's see, knowledge of the one true God, his nature, his plans for creation, his expectations of his creatures, and other things like that) is a commitment to the unity of body and soul. In the early years of the Church, Christianity was in danger of being hijacked by Gnosticism, a set of ideas floating around in the weird and wonderful world of Graeco-Roman religion predating Jesus. The Gnostics believed that the world and matter and bodies were inherently evil and corrupt. They thought that they were somehow stuck down here, trapped in human bodies, but it was all a dreadful mistake and they didn't belong here at all. Those who attained knowledge (*gnosis* is Greek for "knowledge") of their true nature would be able to leave this nasty mess behind and ascend to the *pleroma*—the region of pure spirit that was their true home. When Gnostics first encountered Christianity, they were quick to identify Jesus as a messenger from the Pleroma come to rescue them. Of course, they thought, he was pure spirit and just *appeared* to come in the flesh; he didn't really have a body, didn't really take on human nature, didn't really suffer or die. God would never have let himself get tangled up with something as horrid as matter. (Incidentally, despite what you may have read in *The DaVinci Code*, the Gnostics would have been the very last people in the world to claim that Jesus got married and made real human babies.)

Christians, like Jews and unlike Gnostics, believe that bodies—teeth, digestive tracts, sweat glands, and all— were made by God. Christians go a huge step further than Jews, though, and believe that one human body became the body of God himself, come into his creation to redeem it. Gnosticism, with its negative attitude to the material world, threatened to rip the heart out of the gospel, and the Church had to fight for its life. It is because of the Gnostic threat that John is so passionate when he insists, "We saw him with our eyes! We heard him! We touched him with our hands!" (1 John 1:1, paraphrase) and so strident when he asserts that the God who sent his Son is the same God who made sun and moon and trees and oceans and men and women, and saw that they were good, and came to dwell among them. When I try to get my neighbors to tell me whether keeping kosher is really about the body or about the spirit, they respond with polite confusion, and in their confusion I see some of the strength that

28

enabled the Church to face down the Gnosticism that would have drained it of its lifeblood.

It was not long before the Church decided that, with the coming of Jesus, the rigorous Jewish separation between what is ritually pure and impure had for the most part done its job. So they pared back the food laws and left only the prohibition on blood, which goes all the way back to God's covenant with Noah. But the idea implicit in the laws of kashruth—the conviction that matter and the body are good and that we *are* our bodies, rather than merely spirits inhabiting them—is as true as it ever was, and the way we eat still has important spiritual implications. You don't need to be an Orthodox Jew to know that eating microwave pizza while leaning on the kitchen counter is no good for your body and not much better for your soul. You don't have to avoid bacon like it is poison to realize that gorging yourself into flabby apathy is not a good way to honor your Creator. You don't need to keep separate sinks and sets of plates to sense that there is some perverse alliance between the Gnostics and the advertisers who seduce us into thinking that time spent preparing and eating real food with care, attention, and love is time wasted and that speed and convenience are prime virtues in food. Whatever God intended by forbidding his people certain types and combinations of food, the laws of kashruth make the business of eating the object of religious attention, and offer the human actions of cooking and eating as acts of worship and obedience. The Church still has something, surely, to learn from the food laws it inherited and then left behind.

Another function of the laws of kashruth is to keep Jews from mixing too freely with their Gentile neighbors. To put it in the words of Yaffa, who is seven, "Kosher is because Hashem wants Jewish people to be different from goyish people." Maintaining cultural integrity, keeping the boundaries between Jews and others clear and intact, is central to the essence of Judaism, and boundaries have a habit of dissolving around the dinner table. If you can't go to dinner with the nice Canaanites next door, you are that much less likely to end up adopting their customs, marrying their daughters, and, inevitably, worshiping their gods. The same is true of the nice Catholics next door. This does not mean that our neighbors avoid or shun us. On the contrary, they have welcomed us and they have fed us. Over the course of many convivial evenings, I've become very partial to gefilte fish (not as hard as it may sound to the uninitiated: it's really good), and I like matzoh ball soup so much that I occasionally make my own from the packet. Kosher wine, on the other hand, despite my devoted attempts to acquire a taste for it, still reminds me of Cherry Coke gone flat.

Our neighbors' hospitality, generosity, and good cooking have broken down barriers of strangeness and shyness but have left other barriers perfectly intact. When we get up to go home, replete with nice gefilte fish and not-so-nice kosher wine, we can't say what one usually says when one is a middle-class American who has just had dinner with friends: "Thanks so much; that was lots of fun. Let's do it again soon. I've got a recipe for paella I've been wanting a chance to try. I'll look at the calendar and give you a call later in the week." We all know perfectly well that the next time we eat together will be at their house again, and that if they drop by our place to chat or borrow a hammer or lend a book, we can't even offer them a cup of tea. I used to find it tempting to make polite noises along the lines of, "Gosh, I feel really bad that we can't return the favor . . ." or whatever, but I got over it. If I talked that way, if I acted as if the boundary imposed by kashruth was a nuisance or awkward or embarrassing, if I treated it as a social inconvenience rather than as something fundamental to our friends' identities and to their fidelity to the God we both worship, then I would disrespect both them and their hospitality.

We are grown-ups, so we only go over for dinner when we are invited. The children, however, are in and out of each other's houses constantly. Ours never miss a chance to scrounge food in their friends' kitchens, but the rule for Jewish children who come to play in our home is tap water in paper cups and nothing else. We have installed a Dixie cup dispenser by the sink for this purpose, and some time ago I rashly bought a huge box of Winnie the Pooh cups. These have proven very popular, and now it's not uncommon for visiting children to announce, "We're thirsty!" as soon as they are fairly in the door. Of course, ours get in on the act and refuse to have anything to do with their ordinary plastic cups when their friends are over, and then there are elaborate and occasionally heated debates about who had Eeyore last time and whose turn it is for Piglet. (Piglet, for some reason, is particularly sought-after, despite being palpably nonkosher.)

The littlest kids, who don't quite get it yet, have to be watched, or they will wander into the kitchen and blithely help themselves to apples and cookies. I could teach Pharaoh a thing or two about the hardening of the heart; many are the times I have snatched Fig Newtons out of the reach of a small person who looks at me accusingly, big dark eyes filling with tears, and says, "But I'm *hungry!*" When they get a bit bigger, they try to argue the case: "Catherine had lunch at our house yesterday, so our food is kosher for you, so your food must be kosher for us, so can I have a sandwich, *please?*" The notion that our food just isn't kosher, period, not even for us, they dismiss as obviously absurd. (The technical term for our food is *treif*; literally it means "torn," but the children spit the word out with such contempt that it seems to pack the meanings of "evil," "poisonous," and "gross" into one little syllable.)

We do, in fact, have kosher cake at least once a year, for some birthday or other. We order it from a bakery, and when we go to pick it up, they seal the box shut with stickers that read "Under supervision of the Scranton Orthodox Rabbinate." We get down paper plates, plastic cups, and plastic forks from the top shelf in the pantry, and then our friends come round and we break the seal on the box, cut the cake with a knife they bring with them, and all tuck in. Actually, the kosher bakery is so good that we get all our cakes there, but when it's just us, or when our guests are Catholics or Nazarenes or Episcopalians or secular humanists, we do without the stickers and use our own plates.

4

The Holy God
and His Stiff-Necked People

Our block is an example of America as it should be. We have Jews and Catholics and WASPs and whites and blacks and some great big extended families from India and Indonesia. The grown-ups all exchange friendly greetings, and the kids ride bikes up and down the street and draw on the sidewalks with chalk. If everybody behaved themselves in their dealings with strangers like the people on our block, the world would be a much nicer place than it is. But, to the best of my knowledge, we are the only Gentiles in the neighborhood whose social lives involve buying rabbinically supervised birthday cakes. While it is in the nature of Christianity to stretch itself around other cultures—to claim as its own the best of Greek philosophy or pagan architecture or African music—it is central to the nature of Judaism, at least as it is understood and lived by the Orthodox, to resist outside influence, stick together, and remain largely distinct from the surrounding cultures.

It is no accident that our neighbors dress, speak, act, and eat differently from most of America. To understand why this is so—in fact, to understand most anything about the Orthodox—you have to look to history, because history is where Jews themselves look to understand their identity and their calling. A central theme of the story of the Jews, from the moment God singled out Abraham and promised to make of him a great nation, is holiness. At Mount Sinai God said to the children of Abraham, "You shall be holy, for I the LORD your God am holy" (Lev. 19:2b). The word "holy," *kodesh* in Hebrew, is tricky. We tend to use it, rather vaguely, to mean extra-good, super-spiritual, or even just really, really nice. The original meaning of *kodesh* is actually "separate" or "set apart." When God tells his people that he is holy, he means that he is different—nothing remotely like the gods of the Egyptians or the Canaanites. "My thoughts are not your thoughts," he tells them. "And my ways are not your ways. I am utterly unlike anything you have experienced or could imagine" (Isa. 55:8, paraphrase). If you try to understand the nature of God and decide to worship him by doing what the Egyptians and the Canaanites and everyone else does—creating and bowing down to images—you will get it wrong. No images. Nothing in the world, nothing that can be represented in matter, can adequately communicate God's essence.

Holiness is not only strange; it is dangerous. If you see God, you die. If you touch the mountain where the presence of God has entered our universe, you die. If you panic because Moses, who is the only person who seems to have any idea what is going on, has been up the mountain for forty days, and you need something that you can understand and touch and control, and you pool all your gold and make an image of a calf and worship that, then lots and lots of you die.

So when God says, "I am holy," he doesn't mean "I am nice." And when he says, "You shall be holy," he doesn't mean "You ought to be nice too." He means that, although his people can never imagine or understand him, they are to be *like* him. This is the outrageous job that God gives to the Jews: the job of making manifest in their lives the holiness, purity, absolute justice, mercy, and goodness of God. It is not a job they can begin to do if they care, even a little, about being normal, fitting in, going with the flow. To be holy means precisely to be different: set apart, proudly weird, bizarrely countercultural, and defiantly unlike the business-as-usual world all around them. That is the task that our neighbors have inherited, and they give themselves to it heart and soul.

Throughout the Bible God rails at his people again and again for being stiff-necked—stubborn, disobedient, unbiddable. He threatens them with dreadful consequences, and in the short term the consequences of their stubbornness and disobedience are indeed quite dreadful. But I imagine that when God calls his people "stiff-necked," he feels rather the way I do when I yell at my daughter to get her nose out of that book *right now* and come down to dinner or else: secretly proud and delighted that she is a hopeless bookworm like her old ma. Stubbornness can be inconvenient and exasperating, but it can also be a very useful quality—and it is a quality that God knows his people will need. It's not easy being different, and the stiff necks of the Israelites will, in the long run, be the key to their holiness and to their very survival as a people.

Before the Israelites crossed the Jordan to take possession of the Promised Land, Moses warned them of the temptations ahead. "When you have your own land," he told them, "life will be a lot easier and more secure than it has been in the wilderness. When that happens, when you feel that you can finally relax and enjoy life, don't forget. Don't forget who you were and where you came from. Don't forget who got you out; don't forget who gave you all this; and don't forget what he has commanded you to do. Stick together and remind each other. Put reminders everywhere—on your doorposts and on your hands and on your foreheads—so that never for a minute will you be able to forget. And don't get too comfortable with your new neighbors. Don't marry them; don't adopt their culture; above all, *don't* worship their gods. There is only one God for you, and you must never forget him even for a minute. Raise your children in a world that revolves around remembrance and identity and obedience. It won't be easy, and it will be even harder for your children, who will grow up with ease and stability and comfort. They will fret and complain: 'But why do we have to keep all these rules? Why can't we just be like everybody else?' You will sit them down and tell them, 'Listen, kids, we were slaves. It was horrible, worse than you'll ever know. It was the LORD who set us free and brought us here. We owe everything to him, and these are his rules, and we are going to keep them.'"

I imagine some version of this ancient conversation, the script of which appears in Deuteronomy 6, takes place on our block most days. "I don't care what other people do. We aren't other people. You are not having ice cream, because we had chicken for dinner. You are not riding your bike, because it's Shabbos. You're not wearing that, because it's not *tznius*. We are Jews, and these are the rules that Hashem gave us, and that's final."

A life lived in single-hearted dedication to a high calling, and in rejection of all distractions from that calling, is not an easy one. Many of us, at times when life was tense and the future insecure, have made great resolutions. "If the tests come back from the lab negative," we tell ourselves, "I will never take anything for granted again. I'll quit smoking and go to Church every week and be more patient with the kids. I'll be a different person." When the danger is past, we launch into our new lives full of energy and excitement and gratitude, but after a while we get accustomed to feeling safe. Our acute awareness of how precious and precarious life is grows dimmer, and our old bad-tempered, lazy habits creep back.

This is what happens to us, and it's what happens to the Israelites when they reach the Promised Land. They begin the struggle to stay faithful and obedient and to make manifest in their national life the vision of God's holiness they had been given. There are good times—conquest and stability and blessings. But sooner or later they go and do pretty much everything they were warned not to do. Before you know it, the people are demanding a king, "like other nations," when the whole point is that they are supposed to be *un*like other nations. God, rather ruefully, gives them Saul—a good-looking kid from an unremarkable family. At first he is humble and obedient and grateful, and he remembers where he came from and who made him king. God blesses him: his mind is clear, his enemies fall before him, and Israel is at peace. But eventually he begins to listen to the voice that hisses in his heart, "Says who? I'm the king; I'm in charge here, and I make my own decisions." He then begins a tragic slide into a wilderness of paranoia, sleeplessness, and rage. Saul's story is the human story, the story of Adam and Eve, the story of all of us when we brush off, in irritation, the notion that we are not, in fact, the final authorities on our own lives and deeds. And Saul's dark fate is a foreshadowing of the darkness in Israel's future.

The darkness is still some way off, though. After Saul comes David, the man after God's own heart. His story, up to a certain point, is the same as Saul's: he begins with humility and courage but soon gets so used to the power and privilege of kingship that he abuses them shockingly and betrays both God and his own nature. But David sees what he has done, takes responsibility, and begs God to create a clean heart and renew a right spirit in him. He gives us a powerful language of repentance and humility that is as immediate as it is ancient, and his example is as crucial for Christians' understanding of holiness as it is for Jews'. David's story is the story of the hope that lies beyond darkness.

David's son Solomon asks for and receives from God such wisdom that his fame spreads throughout the nations; during his reign the Temple is built and Israel reaches the height of its power, wealth, and prestige. By now the wilderness years are a long time in the past, and it seems that nothing can threaten Israel, that she will go from strength to strength. To consolidate Israel's supremacy and security, Solomon does what all kings do: he makes allegiances with neighboring kings by marrying their daughters. And in his old age, as wise as he is, his love for his foreign wives turns his heart from exclusive love of God. He drifts so far from the way of holiness into the normal patterns of international politics and diplomacy that he builds shrines to his wives' gods. Solomon's state-sponsored idolatry is a final and fatal violation of the holiness by which Israel stands or falls. So she falls. After Solomon's death the nation splits into two rival kingdoms, and they begin a long descent into chaos, idolatry, corruption, materialism, injustice—becoming more and more like everybody else and less and less like the Holy One.

The prophets, scorching or imploring or bitter, break their hearts trying to get the people to see themselves as God sees them, to understand what they are doing to themselves, and to turn and be healed. But few people listen, and things go from bad to worse. Eventually the northern kingdom is conquered by Assyria, and ten tribes are swallowed up and lost to history. The southern kingdom hangs on longer, but their worship of God is a shallow, ceremonial affair—a far cry from the holiness to which they are called—and is not enough to sustain a society that is increasingly corrupt, materialistic, and hollow. A couple of kings walk in the footsteps of David, making sincere attempts to stop the rot and turn their people back to holiness. But their reforms die with them. Nebuchadnezzar of Babylon sees his chance; he attacks Jerusalem, destroys the Temple, and ravages the land. The survivors are left to starve in the ruins while the Babylonians take the elite—those who know how to build granaries and write poems and compose music and design irrigation systems—back home with them as slaves.

The exiles are far from home, their society devastated, their covenant with God (it must have seemed) finally ruptured. The only sensible thing for them to do is make the best of it: settle down, learn the local customs, learn to think of this foreign land as home, marry Babylonians, worship the local gods, blend in, and try to forget. Some of them probably do. But many refuse to do the sensible thing. They refuse to assimilate, to put the past behind them, to blend into the background—just as our neighbors refuse to give up their odd traditions and their odd clothes and disappear into the melting pot of American culture. The stiff-necked Jews cling stubbornly to their identity and keep alive the memory of the Law, even though they seem to have lost forever the blessings of land and nationhood that the Law was supposed to bring. They remember and are sustained by the words of the prophets, who spoke of the purifying fire of God's anger and also of his enduring love and faithfulness.

They remember and they do not give up hope. When, in one of the strangest reversals of fortune in all of history, Cyrus of Persia conquers the Babylonian Empire and decides to send the captives back to their own land, the Jews in Babylon have no doubt that, whatever Cyrus *thinks* his motives are, he is actually a tool in the hand of a God whom he does not know: the God of Israel, the Holy God who called them to be holy like him. The exiles' return to their home is not easy; their old enemies are not happy to see them back and do everything they can to stop their regaining control of the region. But having overcome all the odds of history, they are not going to let a few hostile armies stop them. Working under enormous pressure, they rebuild the walls and the Temple.

A greater challenge than that of restoring Jerusalem is rebuilding their culture, rededicating themselves to being the holy nation it was their God-given destiny to be. Instead of the magisterial promises and warnings of Moses or the anguish and exultation of the prophets, this time they have as their guide the tireless, vehement harangues of Nehemiah.

Nehemiah is one of my favorite people in the Bible. He has one of the stiffest necks of all time, and he is determined, absolutely determined with every fiber of his being, that Israel is not going to mess up again. Nobody, but nobody, is going to break the Law on his watch. And it's always his watch. He patrols the city, the book of the Law of Moses in hand. He snoops; he bullies; he pokes his nose into people's lives and businesses and bedrooms. Where he finds that things are not being done according to the Law, he sets things straight—immediately and forcefully. He comes across people bringing goods in and out of the city for trade on the Sabbath. He writes:

> Then I remonstrated with the nobles of Judah and said to them, "What is this evil thing that you are doing, profaning the sabbath day? Did not your ancestors act in this way, and did not our God bring all this disaster on us and on this city? Yet you bring more wrath on Israel by profaning the Sabbath. . . . If you do so again, I will lay hands on you." From that time on they did not come on the sabbath. . . . Remember this also in my favor, O my God, and spare me according to the greatness of your steadfast love. (Neh. 13:17–18, 21b, 22b)

No sooner has Nehemiah pushed Israel into proper compliance with Sabbath law than he comes across another problem: one that makes him even angrier. Some of the settlers married women from the surrounding nations and had children who did not even speak Hebrew. With the mortar hardly dry on the Temple, they were already slipping back into laziness, leaving the high and hard calling of kodesh, of being different. This time Nehemiah really loses it.

> And I contended with them and cursed them and beat some of them and pulled out their hair; and I made them take an oath in the name of God, saying, "You shall not give your daughters to their sons, or take their daughters for your sons or for yourselves. Did not King Solomon of Israel sin on account of such women? Among the many nations there was no king like him . . . ; nevertheless, foreign women made even him to sin. Shall we then listen to you and do all this great evil and act treacherously against our God by marrying foreign women?" (Neh. 13:25–27)

This goes deeply against the grain of contemporary America, where we are inclined to admire the courage and creativity needed to build families and communities and traditions out of diverse cultural materials. But my Orthodox neighbors are wholeheartedly on Nehemiah's side. They have not forgotten what Solomon's love for his foreign princesses did to Israel, and they regard intermarriage as a betrayal of their calling, as well as a serious threat to the survival of Judaism.

"Thus I cleansed them from everything foreign," Nehemiah says. "Remember me, O my God, for good"

(Neh. 13:30a, 31b). I love the way Nehemiah reports proudly back to God. He must have gotten on everybody's nerves and made a lot of enemies, but he never for a second doubted that he was doing the right thing: acting in the best interests of the people whom he was cursing and threatening and beating.

I am sure that God does indeed remember Nehemiah. History certainly does. The Judaism that Nehemiah legislated and bullied and nagged into place held and is still holding. Against all logic and reason, and in defiance of all the horrors of history, Jews have survived and remembered who they are, where they came from, and to whom they owe their allegiance. They have remembered and obeyed not just when things went well—when they had cisterns and vineyards and olive groves—but also when they had nothing, when the Temple was destroyed again, when they were driven into exile, when their villages were burnt by laughing Cossacks, when they were locked in ghettos and starved, when they were hoarded into cattle trucks and gas chambers.

All this—the persecution and violence and hatred and suffering—would have ended if only they had been willing to stop being so stubbornly different and just blend in. But their necks are very, very stiff, and once they turned to God, they did not turn away again. And here they are, on my block, in their funny hats and long skirts and wigs, peppering their conversations with strange, guttural foreign words, totally ignoring all the normal things that everybody else does—Christmas shopping, *American Idol*, tank tops, pepperoni pizza with extra cheese—stubbornly and cheerfully weird and countercultural and holy, not the least bit like other people. And a constant reminder to me that the ways of the Holy God are not like our ways.

5

Good Shabbos

Nehemiah got very bent out of shape about violations of
the Sabbath. After he chewed out the nobles of Judah, he
locked down the city at sundown on Friday and posted
guards at the gates. For the first couple of weeks, the mer-
chants camped outside the gates, hoping, presumably, to
pick up some business from passersby. When Nehemiah
found out about this, he threatened them, with his usual
vigor, and they finally got the message. For Nehemiah it was
clear that Israel's failure to observe the Sabbath was one of
the sins that had led to their exile. The commandment
about Sabbath is right up there at the top of the Ten
Commandments, alongside the prohibitions against idolatry and graven images. Once again it is about holiness—
honor the Sabbath and keep it *holy*. Part of Israel's calling to
be a nation utterly unlike other nations is the instruction to
set apart one day—the last day of the week, the day on which
God rested after the work of creation—and to make it
utterly unlike other days.

The separateness of the Sabbath—which runs from sundown on Friday to sundown on Saturday—from the other six days of the week is one of the most distinctive features of Orthodox life. Like every detail of the Torah, the commandment about honoring the Sabbath and keeping it holy has been interpreted and debated and elaborated on through the centuries. The most important bit of interpretation identifies the prohibited work as the thirty-nine activities involved in building the Temple, so on Shabbos (the Hebrew word my neighbors use) you can't do anything that the Jews are recorded as having done while working on the Temple. This rules out writing, sewing, building, washing, buying, selling, carrying, tearing (on Friday night some families take the toilet paper out of the bathroom and put a box of tissues in instead—or so my children tell me; it's not the sort of thing that comes up in conversation if you're older than ten), and thirty-one other things.

The prohibition that probably has the greatest impact is that against kindling a fire. This, in the judgment of the rabbis whose work it has been to guide Jewish life through an ever-changing world, includes anything that creates a spark, including internal combustion engines. The most obvious effect of this is that observant Jews can't drive on Shabbos. The beat-up vans, cluttered with car seats, strewn with cookie crumbs, and occasionally decorated with Yiddish bumper stickers, park on Friday night and don't move for twenty-five hours. The families who crowd into them on the other six days of the week walk to shul in their best clothes. But there's a lot more to it than not driving. Going twenty-four hours in the modern world without using electricity involves a serious reorganization of life. No turning lights on and off, no cooking, no hot water, no telephones. Getting ready for Shabbos is a big rush: a whole day's worth of meals need be cooked and set on a low heat to keep warm, and everybody needs to take showers before the sun goes down. On Friday afternoon the grocery store up the road is full of men with big hats and small children. I can imagine harried women in chaotic kitchens yelling, "Two hours to go and we're out of eggs! Go get some, would you? And we could use some pasta while you're there. And take these kids with you before I step on one of them!"

People make arrangements. Jewish tradition agrees with Jesus that Shabbos is made for man and not man for Shabbos. If you need to take your child to the emergency room, you put her in the car and go without giving it a second thought. And whatever you can do to keep life as smooth as possible is fine. There are timers for lights, special settings on stoves, and so on; so the things that need to get done can, without anybody doing anything that will create a spark.

But occasionally it goes wrong and someone forgets to set the timer or a kid turns on a light in the bedroom or a plate on the stove overheats and starts to look dangerous. This is where *my* family comes in. Every now and then someone will come and knock on our door—of course, they can't ring the bell—to ask us to turn on the furnace or the bathroom light. I love being called on as a Shabbos goy. If I hear the loud telltale knock at the door, I race Glen so I can get there first and be the one to help. Partly it's that I take a childish pleasure in little errands and petty usefulness on any day of the week. More than that, however, I have come to like being part of Shabbos. The day does not enter our neighborhood with the grand drama in which it comes to the Western Wall, but we certainly notice it; we are aware of the sun going down on Fridays in a way we are not the rest of the week. As we unwind at the end of the week, we often find ourselves drifting out onto the porch to watch and wave as people walk by on the way to shul. Shabbos has become part of the rhythm of our lives.

But unless someone needs me to unscrew the bulb in the refrigerator that they forgot about, we rarely see our neighbors on Shabbos. The kids who are in and out of our house all week are not allowed to come because they must be in a "Shabbos house." And although our kids are welcome at their houses, I don't generally let them go, as I can't imagine they wouldn't be in the way. My friends always told me that they love Shabbos, but quite frankly, I never believed them. Until recently I assumed that Shabbos observance was a big nuisance—some sort of penitential thing that Jews had to make the best of and pretended to like for the benefit of outsiders. When someone summoned me as a Shabbos goy, I would do the job, chat for a couple of minutes, and then leave, assuming that they would find it an irritation to have me hanging around watching them navigate all the annoying rules.

My attitude changed suddenly and completely when I stopped by Ahuva's for some reason one Shabbos afternoon. An appetizing smell was coming from the kitchen; Yaakov and Simcha were doing puzzles on the floor; Yosef was bent over a Hebrew book at the table; Dovid was trying to stand on his head. Something about the scene struck me as peculiar, but it took me a minute to figure out what it was. Ahuva has eight children, runs a catering business from home, heads fund-raising for the Day School, works in the *mikveh* every evening from her children's bedtime until her own, and sews most of the clothes for her own family and lots of other people besides. She is perpetually on the move, manhandling toddlers and shopping bags in and out of the car with her sleeves rolled up, flour on her nose, needles stuck through her shirt, and the cell phone clipped to her belt ringing every two minutes. In years I don't think I had ever seen her sit down for three minutes at a time, even during meals. But here she was lying on the sofa with the little ones lolling against her, listening to Dina read a sci-fi novel. She couldn't cook; she couldn't sew; she couldn't shop; she didn't have to answer the phone. She just had to *be*.

It was one of those sudden shifts in perspective, like when you think you have been looking at two black faces on a white background and suddenly all you can see is a white vase on a black background. I had always thought of Shabbos as a twenty-five hour prison of petty regulation, enlivened by a bit of religion. Suddenly I saw why my friends spoke of it with such love, why they thought of the day not as a prison but as a queen, why Ahuva insists that her children spend the day in homes where Shabbos is observed. "There's an atmosphere in a Shabbos house that's not like anything else," she says. It's not just that Ahuva was getting a break from her hectic life, but that she was at the epicenter of a place where restfulness was absolutely palpable: not just an absence of activity but a real presence. Had there been royalty in the house, the atmosphere could not have been more different from the other days of the week.

Of course, we have a holy day too. From the very beginning, Christians met to worship not on the last day of the week, when God rested, but on the first, when Christ rose from the dead. In the fourth century, Sunday was declared to be a day not only of worship but also of rest, and this has been observed in a variety of forms by different bits of Christianity since then. In our family we do try to make it a special day. We go to Mass, and in theory I don't "work" on Sunday. In practice all that means is I don't do the sort of things I do for my job, the one I get paid for. But the break from reading for class, writing lectures, editing articles, and grading papers gives me time to write letters or weed or sew on buttons or pay bills or do some cooking to ease the week ahead or do all the things I put off during the week knowing that Sunday will give me a chance to "catch up." If we ever do get "caught up" and "on top of things" so we can "afford" to take a "day off," it generally involves either preparing a big roast dinner (with Yorkshire pudding, three veggies, and homemade pies as compensation for a week of pasta) or packing lunches, diapers, and changes of clothes and loading the car to head out to do something a lot less restful than sitting in my nice quiet office "working." Really, our Sunday "rest" is not much more than a minor reshuffling of work—a break from routine but still a calculated part of accomplishing everything that my life demands I accomplish.

Why, exactly, do I have so much to do? The easiest answer is that I am acceding to the demands of a high-paced, competitive, technological, efficiency-obsessed culture and allowing it to drown out my need for spiritual tranquility. Now there's a lot in that, and it is quite bad enough. But high-paced efficiency-obsessed cultures do not create themselves. David Dawson suggests a challenging and rather sinister answer to the question of why we are so busy. "Though we say that we yearn for more free time," he says,

> we avoid it like the plague, preferring instead to seek out periods of leisure time, during which we can pursue leisure activities. And if we are successful, if we can keep the calendar full and time moving under our control, we can continue to live as though we believed our greatest illusion—that we are immortal.[1]

If Dawson is right—and I'm rather afraid he is, at least in my case—then our obsessive busyness is a way of distracting ourselves from our mortality, our contingency, from the fact that our world and our lives are not our own. He suggests that simply paying attention to life as it is, rather than striving to maintain the illusion of mastery over it, would be transformative. I know that he is right. I had a spiritual director once who made me spend half an hour a day sitting. Not reading or praying or meditating on a Bible passage—just sitting. I hated it. I was bored and anxious all at once, and I probably snuck a look at the clock forty times in thirty minutes. But somehow during the short months I actually kept up the discipline, the rest of my life really was different: I was calmer, my mind clearer, less cluttered by anxieties and resentments and fantasies. Then something minor—I can't remember what—changed in the circumstances of my life, and I seized on it as an excuse to stop the tedious discipline of freeing time and sitting with it.

Now, of course, I have myriad excuses, which I recite to myself like a mantra (a full-time job, a marriage, four kids, a house that is a perpetual work in progress, and at present a book to write), and I am no closer to taking half an hour to let time be free than I am to training for a marathon. I even multitask prayer, folding it into the kids' bedtime, so I can cross "Provide positive spiritual role model," "Spend quality time with children," and "Cultivate relationship with my Lord and Savior" off my "things to do" list with one efficient sweep of the pen. This, of course, is blatant cheating: quite staggeringly dishonest, really, but I have *such* good excuses, *such* a lot I have to get done.

Ahuva's life places just as many demands on her and then some, but the commandment to honor the Sabbath and keep it holy trumps everything else. And the commandment means that she, all her family, the four other Orthodox families on our block, and all Shabbos-observant Jews everywhere spend the time from sundown Friday to sundown Saturday inhabiting time and space in a way that is quite unique. The job of the Shabbos laws is to prevent Jews from making any changes to the world, from tinkering with what God made for the space of one day. For one day they simply have to live in the world as it is and cede control to God. All the laws, the thirty-nine acts that generations of rabbis have multiplied into hundreds of prohibitions on the most trivial everyday activities, are an adamantine edge to chisel holiness into the week in a way that cannot be ignored or evaded by distraction and must therefore be welcomed and embraced and celebrated. There is no way to cheat, catch up, get ahead, achieve, manage, accomplish, or do anything at all except experience time as creatures whom God has made in his own image and blessed and chosen and called.

It would be nice, wouldn't it, if at this point I could write that we have embraced a sort of Shabbos of our own: that after my revelation about the beauty of a holy day, I have led the family into allowing Sunday to be a day of real rest and beauty. If we had, I have no doubt it would be wonderful. If three hours a week of getting-nothing-done turned down the flame under my compulsion to fret and nag and accomplish, I can only imagine what twenty-five hours might do. It hasn't happened. I am still a dedicated fretter and nagger and accomplisher. But nowadays I am drawn to Shabbos houses, to time that is truly free, to space that, under the guidance of Torah, is set apart to welcome holiness.

I still feel awkward about hanging around on Shabbos, mind you. No longer because I think that my friends will be embarrassed by having me around to see what a pain in the neck Shabbos is, but because I am embarrassed to bring my usual compulsive self into a space that is not usual. Nonetheless, I am drawn to Shabbos houses; I look for excuses to drop round and angle for invitations to go over to play Scrabble. (Scrabble doesn't violate the prohibition on writing because all you are doing is rearranging tiles. Keeping score would be a problem, however, because writing down numbers on paper would involve making permanent marks, thus creating something new, and even God did not create on the seventh day. But as Shabbos was made for man and not man for Shabbos, we don't let that stop us; we each get a book and keep score by putting bookmarks in the pages.) Maybe something of it will rub off on me, and in a few years—when everyone is out of diapers, and I've finished those syllabi on missiology and science and religion I've been toying with for years, and I've finally written my book on Victorian religious historiography— I'll get the point, learn to stop being efficient and over-achieving, and, for a few hours, simply be God's creature.

6

Why Is This Night
Unlike All Other Nights?

M y family is welcome in the sacred space and time of Shabbos. We can eat in sukkahs and go to brissim and bar mitzvahs and *shalom zachors* and parties for Purim or Hanukkah. The only place our neighbors will never invite us, for complicated *halakhic* reasons, is the Seder on the first night of Pesach.

The story of Passover, in Exodus, is familiar to Christians. The glory days when Joseph was Pharaoh's right-hand man and his brothers were honored guests in Egypt are four hundred years in the past, as far distant from their descendants as Shakespeare and the *Mayflower* are from us. The children of Israel have been slaves for generations, and now they are subject to a ghastly policy of state-ordered infanticide. In the midst of brutal oppression, they have somehow kept alive the old stories; they remember Abraham and the God who called him and gave him a new name and the promise of a land of his own. But the promises seem to be going nowhere fast, and Abraham's God must seem about as real and powerful as the tooth fairy compared to the huge and haughty gods of the Egyptians, who gave *their* followers wealth and power, who look down from massive pillars at the suffering Hebrews. But God is waiting. He sees and hears and bides his time. And then a fugitive in the desert, who before he was a fugitive was a prince in Egypt, and before that was the child of a slave, comes across a burning bush and is transformed yet again. This time he is a prophet, changed by the voice of the God of Abraham, Isaac, and Jacob, who has come blasting out of the old stories to rescue his people.

It's a dark and dreadful story, one of burning pride and icy stubbornness, of violence, terror, and destruction. It is also a joyful story of fidelity and salvation and freedom. The darkness and the joy come together at Pesach, when the Angel of Death kills the firstborn of every Egyptian family and passes over the houses—their doors smeared with blood—where the slaves are eating a meal of lamb and unleavened bread. They come together again on the shores of the Red Sea, where the Israelites look back at the waters closing over their pursuers and sing a hymn praising God for his steadfast love and guidance and for his terrifying power. He is a mighty warrior: his fury consumes his enemies like fire burning stubble.

Jews remember this dark, triumphant, painful, joyful story every spring. The preparation starts weeks earlier with a housecleaning of mind-blowing thoroughness. The

Israelites ate unleavened bread at the meal of Passover for the simple reason that they were in a hurry and there was no time for the bread to rise. Now, in remembrance, my friends track down every trace of yeast, not just the obvious stuff in the pantry and the remainders of the sandwich that the eight-year-old snuck upstairs when nobody was looking, but every last speck of anything in corners and carpets that might possibly have been in contact with leavening of any sort. All the plates and pots and knives and forks have to be sealed up and put in the basement, and plates and pots and knives and forks that have never touched anything leavened are taken out and put into freshly scrubbed kitchen cabinets. During the eight days of Pesach, a whole extra layer of food laws comes into play. Everything has to be not only kosher, but kosher for Pesach, which means that it is certified to have not an atom of yeast in it. Apart from anything else, this gets awfully expensive as it eliminates most of the supermarket foods that are all right the rest of the year; corn syrup, for instance, is kosher, but not for Pesach.

When everything is cleaner than my house has ever been, at least since I've lived in it, the Seder comes—the re-enactment of the Hebrews' last meal as slaves. Everything is prescribed down to the smallest detail. Although it is a festive meal, cooked at home and eaten around the family table, the ritual element is so strong that it is more like a liturgical celebration than like, say, Thanksgiving. By and large on Thanksgiving one eats turkey and green bean casserole and that strange concoction with sweet potatoes and marshmallows. But if you don't care for turkey, there's no real reason you can't have sushi. At a Seder, not only the six symbolic dishes, but even the way they are arranged on the table and the order in which they are eaten, are prescribed by both time-honored tradition and law. At Thanksgiving, again, it is generally regarded as a good idea for someone to take a few minutes to quiz the little ones on the story of the Pilgrims and the Indians, and if you come from a certain sort of family, you may well take turns talking about what you are thankful for. But if you prefer to talk about sports or politics or books, then there's nothing to stop you. At a Seder there's a little book by every seat with the script for the conversation, which is a theological commentary on the meal itself. As they eat, they read, question, discuss. The aim is for those present to identify so completely with the experience of their ancestors that the thousands of years between them vanish and they feel as if they are there, in Egypt, on the brink of freedom. The Seder, then, is thoroughly ritualized and deeply regular; it links the Jews to a story that is in the past and, therefore, cannot change.

Jesus's disciples must have looked forward eagerly to their Seder. It had been a rough week. Jerusalem was swarming with pilgrims at the holidays. The authorities were on alert, and the usual tensions were raised to a heightened pitch. There were a lot of tensions in Roman-occupied Judea. The Romans cultivated a public image of liberalism and tolerance, but everybody knew that the image was a thin veneer over the brutal realities of imperial expansion and military power. If they felt that their dominance was being challenged in any way, they turned very ugly very quickly. Too much public grumbling about taxes, rumors of subversive groups, urban guerillas plotting rebellion, and out came the crosses and nails.

Jews responded to this situation in different ways. The priestly classes had the task of trying to maintain the integrity of Temple worship, offering pure sacrifices and prayer to a jealous God who tolerated no rivals, while staying on the right side of an empire so arrogant that they were on the verge of honoring their emperor as a god. The Pharisees worked among the common people, trying to help them to observe the Law scrupulously and to maintain absolute fidelity to God while staying under the radar of the Romans. Others were less ready to be patient; some denounced the whole structure, priests and Pharisees, as hopelessly contaminated by their compromises with the Romans, so they took off to the desert to worship in purity. Others dreamed of rising up and forcibly taking back their land from the hands of the Romans. All watched and hoped for Moshiach, the one whom God had promised through the prophets to send them.

This is why, when Jesus and the disciples arrived in Jerusalem earlier that week to the kind of welcome generally reserved for military conquerors, the Pharisees had pleaded with him to get the crowd to simmer down and go home before the Romans decided they needed to deal with the disruption themselves. Jesus calmly ignored them. Then, on their first visit to the Temple, he lost his temper, raging about thievery and smashing things. Next he established *himself* in the Temple, as if it were his own house, and publicly accused the religious authorities of being hypocrites, of acting out of love for their own status rather than love for God and Torah. Small wonder that the priests' and Pharisees' nervous suspicions quickly hardened into deadly hostility. They decided that Jesus had to be killed. He knew it, and let them know that he knew it, but it didn't slow him down.

It must have been very frightening for the disciples. After three years with Jesus, of course, they were no strangers to controversy. But this was on an altogether different scale from dinner table debates with irritated Pharisees in fishing villages. Besides, Jesus had been saying weird and disturbing things recently. He had more or less admitted that he was the Messiah, and their hearts leapt and their minds filled with visions of fame and glory. But he dumped ice water on their fantasies. "Yes, I'm the Messiah. And it's not what you think. It's going to get really ugly, and I'm going to die. Do you get this, guys? Are you even listening? You need to be ready for this. They're going to kill me. And you know what else? They're going to kill you too."

So they must have looked forward eagerly to Pesach. They found an upstairs room somewhere and made arrangements for the Seder. At least that one evening would be safe and calm and predictable. It would be just them, and they all had their parts to play, their familiar lines to say. Even Jesus, even as strange as he had been recently, couldn't mess with Pesach, could he?

But, of course, Jesus does mess with Pesach. In his hands the unleavened bread is no longer just a reminder that their ancestors had to leave in a hurry. It is his body, he tells them, and it will be broken. The wine is no longer the blood of the lamb that kept the Angel of Death at bay. It is *his* blood, and it will be spilled, and they have to drink it. This Seder is no longer a story that is familiar and safe and comforting. This Seder is about the present, the turbulent, unpredictable present, and even more frightening, it is about a strange new future in which people will do what the disciples are doing and will remember this evening and reenact this meal in catacombs and palaces and barns and fields and living rooms and soaring cathedrals and tiny whitewashed Churches. All moments, past and future, are centered on this moment and on Jesus himself. And then Judas dips his bread in the cup and leaves, and Jesus goes out to the garden, and over the next three days the story of Passover and the freeing of the Jews is turned inside out, into the story of Easter and the redemption of all creation.

The situation is, of course, more complicated than that. Christianity is built on the foundation of the Jewish covenant, but it is not just slapped on top of it like a trailer home onto a concrete lot. Christian theology draws freely, indeed rather cavalierly, on the whole of the Old Testament, and while the links between Jewish and Christian festivals are a good place to start, they do not tell the whole story. At that strange, frightening Seder, when Jesus said that the bread and wine were his body and blood for the forgiveness of sins, he was putting himself in the place not only of the lambs of the first Passover, but also of the scapegoats that were driven out to the desert every year bearing the sins of Israel, and of the lambs, doves, bulls, grain, and oil that were offered in the Temple in accordance with the Law, and of the ram caught in the thicket by its horns that God provided to take the place of Isaac. The days that follow this strange new Seder, days the Church keeps as its holiest days, echo the themes of Yom Kippur, or the Day of Atonement (the holiest day in the Jewish year), and Pesach. When Christians think about the story of Jesus and then look back at the Old Testament, we see shadows and glimpses and hints—the technical term is *types*—everywhere we turn.

The intimate connection in the meanings of Jewish and Christian rituals and symbols can be surprising when the two religions live side by side as they do in my neighborhood. I got quite a start once when Ahuva casually dropped into the conversation the phrase "paschal lamb." For Catholics the phrase is absolutely bursting at the seams with theological, symbolic, and spiritual significance: the Lamb who was slain, the Lamb of God who takes away the sins of the world. I was momentarily bewildered by the sudden turn in the conversation, and then I realized that she wasn't talking about theology at all; she was talking about food. *Paschal lamb? It's what the Hebrews ate at Pesach, of course.* I hazarded a quick explanation of what Christianity does with Passover, and when I got to the bit about the Eucharist, she reacted with palpable embarrassment, as if the whole body-and-blood thing were a skeleton in the Christian closet, something that everybody knows about but that people generally have the good taste not to speak of in public. The disciples certainly found the command to eat the flesh and drink the blood of Jesus shocking and unsettling. Maybe Christians should too.

As tightly interwoven as Easter and Passover are, theologically and symbolically, they don't always happen at the same time. There's a complicated business about solar and lunar cycles and the switch from the Julian to the Gregorian calendar and things of that sort. The two festivals can be as much as four weeks apart, but I like it when they coincide, when our neighbors are scrubbing their houses at the same time that we are fasting for Lent. When we are getting into the car to go to Maundy Thursday Mass to remember the Last Supper, I like to know that the Rubins and the Gindoffs and the Schwartzes and the Cohens are in their houses doing what the disciples thought they were going to do when Jesus turned it all on its head. It is the sharpest reminder of how very close we are—and how very far. We are remembering the same stories, the actions of the same God, but our relations to the stories are different, and the way we remember them is different.

As it happens, I have actually been to a Passover Seder at a Church in Virginia, years before I had even been in the same room as an Orthodox Jew. It was interesting and educational and done in a spirit of respect for Judaism and Jews. There are a number of reasons why it is important for Christians to understand Passover, and there are plenty of Churches that host Seders, and I can quite see their point. But it made me somewhat uncomfortable at the time, and does so now more than ever. When I tentatively mentioned the subject to an Orthodox friend, she obviously didn't like it one bit. She felt, I imagine, rather as I would feel if I heard that a group of ecumenically minded, well-intentioned, open-hearted Muslims or Buddhists had bought a book and got together to celebrate the Eucharist. I certainly wouldn't hold it against them personally, but I'd really prefer they didn't.

The story of Passover as it is enacted at the Seder is a family story, and as such is very personal. It wasn't the ancestors of the Virginia congregation who smeared blood on the door frames of their huts, ate a hurried meal with all their possessions in bundles at their sides, clutched their children as wails of anguish streamed from the houses of their oppressors, and took off into an unknown freedom in pursuit of an almost-forgotten God who had remembered them just in time. When the Angel of Death swept over Egypt, our ancestors were getting on with their business in Ireland and Sweden and Africa and England, quite unaware that in a distant desert an unknown God was taking history by the throat and calling to his side the people he had chosen for his own. It would be many centuries before God made himself a child of Israel, took the story of the Exodus by the throat, and gave it to us and to the whole world.

Actually, this year some new friends, Reform Jews who have quite a different take on this issue (as on many others), have invited us to their Seder. I feel rather shy about it, and a little bit worried that our Orthodox friends will disapprove: but only a *very* little bit, and certainly not enough to return anything other than an enthusiastic, "Oh, *can* we? I didn't know! Gosh, thanks, we'd love to come."

7

Train Up a Child
in the Way He Should Go

A contraband ring was broken up recently at the yeshiva—the Hebrew boys' high school. A list of clients, schedules, and a complicated system of concealment, including alarms that could be rigged to the dorm doors, were discovered in the possession of Yosef, the ringleader, my friend's eldest son, and quite the most charming lad you could wish to meet. The object of all this criminal ingenuity? Marijuana? Pornography, perhaps? Liquor or cigarettes at the very least? Nope. Two tattered Harry Potter books that were being passed around according to a strict rota.

A world in which rebellious teenaged boys can satisfy their need to transgress boundaries, defy authority, and damn the torpedoes by reading high-quality children's literature is, I suspect, a world rather different from the one most American teenagers inhabit. But the world in which the yeshiva students are being trained to take their part as adults is different from that inhabited by most Americans, and the point of education is, after all, to equip young people for what awaits them in adulthood. As most of my waking hours are spent in some sort of activity involving the education and formation of young people—raising my own little flock and teaching theology to college kids—I find it intriguing, and sometimes challenging, to watch my friends' children growing up in the world—very different from mine—of Orthodox Judaism.

The process starts very young—it has to. At the age of thirteen for boys and twelve for girls (they say that girls are more mature, and who am I to argue?), young people become bar or bat mitzvah, which means they take upon themselves responsibility—up to then assumed by their parents—for obeying the commandments. There are a lot of commandments, and obeying them is a serious business, so by the time children become adults, you want the obedience to be second nature. As soon as kids can toddle, they are shown how to touch the mezuzah on doorposts as they go through doors. As soon as they start putting words together, they begin to learn the *berakhas*, the proper blessings to say in Hebrew before eating fruit or drinking water or after washing their hands.

They dress distinctively from an early age. Men keep their heads covered to remind them that God is above them. For little boys up to the age of three, this means long hair; the first Orthodox "event" we attended was watching as Dovid lost his shaggy glam-rocker locks and got his first yarmulke. Our Adam, a lone boy in a sea of sisters, has grown up thinking of yarmulkes as the badge of masculinity; we eventually had to get him his own to prevent him from nabbing Dovid's. Women, it is said, are closer to God than men are (again, who am I to argue?) and in consequence don't need yarmulkes. They are, however, subject to laws and traditions about behavior (women cannot, for instance, sing, dance, or act in the presence of men) and about dress (married women cover their hair with snoods or wigs or hats). This also starts young; even teeny little girls wear long skirts, long sleeves, and high necks in irreproachably opaque fabrics, even when it is 95 degrees in the shade. Needless to say, the purpose of the dress code—the term is *tznius*—is modesty, although I am here to tell you, in case you don't already know, that the average active little girl is a great deal more modest in leggings or overalls than in a skirt.

Through eighth grade the Orthodox kids all go to the Hebrew Day School just down the road from us, where the playground is always full of little boys with flying tzitzis playing baseball. Half the day they study "English" subjects, meaning not only English but also math, history, social studies, and so on, and the other half is dedicated to "Hebrew": the language itself and subjects like *Chumash*, the books of Moses; *Novi*, the Prophets; *loshon*, proper speech; *hashkafa*, ethics; and *halakha*, how to observe the mitzvahs as outlined in the Talmud. Sex education is not included in either half of the curriculum. In the most strictly observant families, young people do not learn how babies are made until they are on the verge of marriage, or so the story goes. I am, I have to say, deeply skeptical about this. Children are experts in the rapid and efficient diffusion of information; it only takes one ten-year-old to pick up the facts from somewhere, and everybody in town under the age of fourteen will know all about it by lunchtime tomorrow and have sworn a solemn oath never to let on to the grown-ups.

Whatever they do or don't know in theory, they don't get a chance to practice. When a boy turns thirteen and becomes a bar mitzvah, he trades in his jeans and T-shirt for a black suit and a white shirt, and tops his yarmulke with a broad-brimmed black hat. (It has to be said, few things set the inherent geekiness of your typical teenage boy into higher relief than does a uniform of wispy side-burns, black suit, and big hat.) Then he vanishes into the yeshiva, where he studies for about a thousand hours a week (a full, although I imagine rather idiosyncratic, high school curriculum *and* a full religious curriculum). Meanwhile, the girls, demure and gorgeous in long pleated skirts and prim white blouses, go to Bais Yaakov, and they see very, very little of the boys.

Men and women have separate hours in the swimming pool at the Jewish Community Center, and kids go to single-sex summer camps with kosher kitchens. I took my daughters to the JCC for the closing ceremony of the girls' bat mitzvah camp this year, because Alizah was directing the closing entertainment program. Alizah is big sister to Yaffa and Ester, and where Yaffa and Ester go, my Catherine and Elisabeth want to go. So we went. It was lovely and so weird that I found it genuinely disorienting. There was the kind of emotional atmosphere you would expect from a bunch of teenagers who had been living together, and presumably sleeping only five hours a night, for a couple of weeks and were beside themselves with exhilaration and exhaustion. There were adorably sincere and goofy sketches on the spiritual theme of the camp, and choruses with recorded backing music, and lots of swaying and arms in the air. There was an antediluvian public address system that shrieked and roared and held up the proceedings for twenty minutes while people fiddled with knobs. There were interminable thank-yous and a blurry video of camp highlights that was hilarious, touching, and deeply meaningful to the girls themselves and totally incomprehensible to everybody else.

What made it so disorienting was how intensely familiar it all was to me. Other than the absence of men, it was in all respects—goofy sketches, choruses, uncooperative PA system, hugging, giggling, in-jokes—identical to the gospel coffeehouses and evangelistic events that were a significant part of my adolescence. Except that we were all fired up about Jesus, and these girls were all fired up about the Torah. I don't know when I've had a more fascinating evening.

Once the years of yeshiva and summer camps are behind them, it is more or less time to start thinking about marriage. Marriages are not arranged in the sense that, say, traditional Hindu marriages are, and *Fiddler on the Roof* matchmakers in head scarves have morphed into professional dating services, but the process of choosing partners is a good deal more formal and includes a great deal more community involvement than in mainstream American society. Dating is not an end in itself; it is a way of looking for a spouse. Dates between young people are arranged by adult family and friends, are in very public places, and serve the purpose of letting people figure out if they want to get married.

During dating and engagement, couples are expected to be *shomrei negiyah*, which means that they have no physical contact. This is not a euphemism for no sex; it really means no physical contact, of any sort, at all. After they are married, they will be *shomrei yichud*, which means they will never again be alone with anyone of the opposite sex, other than a close relation. (Or a doctor, or dentist, or if your husband is out and the guy finally shows up to fix the furnace, you let him in. They're strict; they're not stupid.)

At social events men and women will separate and sit on opposite sides of the room. This practice, I have to say, drives me nuts. For one thing, it goes without saying that the wailing infants, the overstimulated toddlers, and the bored, sulky ten-year-olds are never, *ever* on the men's side. For another, the talk on the men's side is all about theology and Scripture—there's usually a rabbi who gives a little speech about the religious significance of the occasion—and on the women's side, largely about domestic matters. Now, I'm no bra-burning bluestocking; I can talk about babies and food with the best of them. But I like theology too, and whatever the men are talking about always sounds so *interesting* (all the more so from being heard in snatches, the way a garden always looks enticing and mysterious if you glimpse it from a moving car). Whenever we go to a "do," I always edge as close as I decently can to the men's side, strain to pick up as much of the conversation as possible, and interrogate my husband afterward to fill in the gaps.

As exasperating as yichud is to someone like me, accustomed to a culture where it is acceptable to talk freely to most everybody about most everything, the reason for it is clear. It's a simple, radical solution to a serious problem. There is a halakhic principle called "building a fence around the Torah," according to which if something is prohibited, you avoid not only it but anything that might possibly bring you into contact with it. That way you can be sure. If you don't even touch money on Shabbos, you can't buy or sell. If you keep separate plates for milk and meat, you can be sure that you will never, by accident, eat a goat that has been cooked in its mother's milk.

By the same token, if you keep daylight between you and all members of the opposite sex from puberty onwards, your chances of starting marriage unhampered by a messy sexual history are excellent. If you never have the chance to fall into conversation with someone at a party and discover that you both love Dickens *and* anchovy pizza *and* Joni Mitchell, or that he gets your sense of humor in a way that your husband, bless his heart, just never has, then it reduces practically to nil the chances that you will ever find yourself caught in the kind of emotional tempest that makes shipwreck of so many hearts, families, and communities.

Family life is extraordinarily important in Judaism, even more than it is in Christianity. This is because Christianity has, from early in its history, accorded high respect to those who, like Paul, choose not to marry in order to devote all of their energy to the service of God. There is no place for voluntary celibacy in Judaism, and much of the service that God requires of Jews is conducted in the family home. The Orthodox regard marriage and family as a universal calling, and many of their laws reflect this.

Chastity, of course, is not the only nor the most important virtue, and sex and marriage are among many things that responsible parents try to prepare their children for in their adult lives. But sex is probably one of the things that parents fret about most, and it is also one of the areas in which the differences between our Orthodox friends and ourselves are most apparent. We all want the same things for our children; we want them to be kind, virtuous, self-assured, devout, faithful, happy people with stable relationships. But we want them to be happy and virtuous and devout in very different worlds. The Orthodox world has a coherent set of practices and institutions to form their young people and a tightly knit community that supports it. Rules and conventions as strict as tznius, negiyah, and yichud, if they are to operate in ways that are healthy rather than neurotic and oppressive, cannot function in the context of individual families. If you are going to raise your children to stay clear of all relationships with the opposite sex except those with their spouses or, briefly, people they are seriously considering marrying, then you need to provide them with a world in which they can follow the rules and still be normal. They need a world in which not only you but the parents of most everybody they know take it for granted that they will socialize only in large groups; a world that is sufficiently tight-knit so that everybody knows everybody, and sufficiently different from the larger world so that it is really impossible for you to blend in; a world set apart from the world of MTV and Abercrombie and Fitch and all the weird things that start to seem almost normal when you're around them enough.

On the one hand, a close-knit, integrated community in which children can grow up securely surrounded by people who reinforce the same commitments is a thoroughly excellent thing. There are many things about the world of the Orthodox that I envy. But it is not our world. And I have mixed feelings about it. This type of stability comes at a very high price, because in contemporary urban America any really homogenous community, whether Jewish or Christian, must of necessity be artificial, since contemporary America is full of all sorts of people. And artificially homogenous communities are necessarily sustained, to some extent, by a "fortress mentality," and the fortress mentality—of fear, suspicion, and even hostility toward the world outside—is something I really don't like. There is, to be sure, plenty to be fearful, suspicious, and hostile about, but there is also plenty that is beautiful and fascinating and challenging and exciting and good, and I want to teach my children to be open to it. I want them to be faithful Christians who live with integrity and in communion with the Church, and I want them to become sophisticated, well-informed, discerning people who are at ease in the world and are open to trusting friendships with people very different from themselves. I want an awful lot, I know, but there it is.

Our kids already live in a rather larger world than their Jewish friends, and the difference between their lives will grow greater as they grow older. For the Orthodox, the teen years represent the phase between childhood and marriage. For our children they will represent the warmup to the extended adolescence of higher education. In ten years Yaffa will be thinking seriously about choosing a husband, and Catherine will be thinking seriously about choosing a college. Yaffa will be going on dates and asking young men with fuzzy beards and big hats about their views on family life. Catherine will be going on campus tours and asking admissions staff about library hours and majors. A couple of years after that, Yaffa will be preparing for her first baby—boy or girl? Catherine will be preparing for junior year abroad—Paris or Tokyo? I am acutely aware that it is one thing to expect your children to keep all the mitzvahs when everybody around them is doing it, and to shomrei negiyah until they are eighteen or nineteen and ready for marriage. It is quite another to expect them to read the Bible and pray when they are in Bhutan for a year with the Peace Corps, and to be chaste and continent through their midtwenties while they are too busy studying and traveling and having adventures to think about marriage. Glen and I are asking a lot.

So, as we think hard about how we can best prepare our children to live good, happy lives, we watch the cohesiveness of the community around us somewhat wistfully. They have resources that are simply not available to us. But while the cohesiveness of the sort of Orthodox Judaism practiced by our neighbors is its great strength, and a strength that we cannot reproduce in our own family, it is a liability as well because it comes as a package. Either our friends' children will follow in the footsteps of their parents and live lives ordered in almost every detail by obedience to the mitzvahs they took on at the cusp of the teenage years, or else they will kick over the traces and go do something altogether different. Most things about Orthodoxy are nonnegotiable; it is an all-or-nothing proposition.

So, in its own way, is Christianity, but it does not come with a ready-made, all-enveloping culture. The nonnegotiable element in Christianity is fidelity to Christ. Of course, everybody needs a culture—humans cannot be human without culture and symbols and companions. But Christ can be—has been—at the center of many different cultures, and our children, as they move into the big wide world, will have the freedom to choose whether to follow Christ in suburban kitchens or monasteries or corner offices, whether to worship him with Latin masses and rosary novenas or with tongues and tambourines, whether to lead lives of fertility and domesticity or austere lives dedicated to prayer and contemplation, whether to stand in solidarity with the oppressed against the great ones of the earth or to be quiet witnesses for justice within the system, whether to wear business suits or overalls or uniforms or tie-dye. The freedom of the children of God may be glorious, but it is also a little dizzying.

The job of Jewish parents is to raise children who will embrace a Torah life in all its dimensions. Our job as Christian parents is to raise our children to follow Christ. So we take them to Church and to Sunday school and to prayer groups, and we read the Bible and pray at home. But it is also our job to prepare them for the glorious and dizzying freedom of Christianity: to teach them how to discern the difference between what is negotiable and what isn't. So we read books with them and watch movies and visit museums and spend time with friends, and talk and talk and listen and listen and talk some more about good and evil, beauty and ugliness, choices and character, and habit and virtues and stories. When puberty hits our household like a hurricane—about five years and counting—we will encourage hobbies and sports and homework, make sensible rules about clothes and dates and sleepovers and curfews, and pretend to shrug it off when we are accused of being vile tyrants; all the things that sensible middle-class American parents do to steer their children through the shoals of adolescence. But we will try to remember that Jesus was not a sensible middle-class American and that they don't have to be either. And we hope that when they are in the throes of their teen years, they will still be as close to Yaffa and Ester as they are now, if only so that when they wail, "But *everybody* else is doing it," we will be able to say, "No, they're not, and you know it!"

8

Not a Jot nor a Tittle

Fifty days after Pesach comes Shavuos, when Jews remember the giving of the Torah on Mount Sinai, the Torah that seals the covenant between them and the God who chose them. When God first made the covenant, he promised Abraham more descendants than there are stars in the sky, and now at Sinai Abraham's descendants gather at the foot of the mountain. God promises them a land of their own, and then they are free and on their way to the Promised Land. God told Abraham that he would make of him a *great* nation. Thus, the greatness to which Israel is called is bound to the Torah; by obedience to the Law, they will make manifest to the world knowledge of the one true God.

The Torah remains the center of Jewish identity. Without the shape it gives to their lives, the Jews could not possibly have survived what history has thrust on them. When the Temple was destroyed and they were thrown out of Jerusalem, it became the anchor of Jewish life. Wherever the bereaved, scattered Jews went then and in the centuries to come—to Spain and Ethiopia and Poland and Iraq—the Torah went. It is a vital, active presence in the lives of our Orthodox neighbors: modern people with camera-phones and minivans and jobs as hairdressers, account-ants, doctors, and caterers. They study it constantly; they obey it; they shape every day, every hour, almost every word and action, around it.

When God promised Abraham descendants, land, and greatness, he also said that through him all the nations of the earth would be blessed. Christians understand this to mean that while God, through the Torah, was shaping the sons of Abraham into a great and holy nation, he was preparing a place where he himself would come into the world, into time and space and history, into human birth and life and death, and draw humans with him into what lies beyond death.

Fifty days after Jesus's shattered, shattering Seder, after he ordered his disciples to drink the blood of the new covenant and then went out to his death, Jerusalem was again full of pilgrims come from far and wide to celebrate Shavuos. The day must have had special resonances for the disciples. Like their ancestors, they had recently passed through the waters of terror and triumph and watched their God demolish the powers of death and darkness. Like their ancestors, they were facing a hostile and uncer-tain world. And, like their ancestors, they were the bear-ers of promises they did not fully understand. Jesus had told them that he had to leave them, that a helper would come, that they held the keys to the kingdom of heaven, that they must go to the end of the earth and baptize and make disciples, and that they would stand before emperors and he would give them the words to say. But as of yet no help had come, and they were as inadequate to the task they had been given as the newly escaped slaves at the foot of Mount Sinai were to the job of building a great nation. They huddled together, prayed, and waited.

What happened next was as strange and frightening as what had happened at Mount Sinai. Back then, Moses had disappeared into a rumbling, flashing cloud on top of the mountain and emerged with the tablets of the Law. Now, fire and roaring wind came to the disciples and rested on them, filled the room, and filled them. The disciples spoke out in words not their own, as Jesus had promised they would, and an astonished crowd quickly gathered. Peter, his lungs swelling with the breath of God, stood up and spoke to the crowd. On that day three thousand people came to faith in Jesus the Messiah and were baptized. On that Shavuos the Church was born. The Greek-speaking Jews present called the festival Pentecost, and this became the Church's term. Shavuos is the seed of Pentecost in the same way that Pesach is the seed of Good Friday and Easter. On Shavuos God gave the Torah that makes Jews into Jews, and on Pentecost he sent the Spirit that makes Christians into Christians. The Christian festivals soak up meaning and symbol from the rich soil of the past and bring forth strange and wonderful new flowers.

The relation between the Torah that Moses brought down from the mountain and the Spirit that descended in tongues of fire becomes a central theme for Christian thought. Paul says that "the letter kills, but the Spirit gives life" (2 Cor. 3:6). He says that to live by the Law is slavery and to live by the Spirit is to live freely as loving children. He even says that those who rely on the works of the Law are under a curse, and that Christ redeemed us from the curse of the Law. These phrases are deep in the Christian consciousness and have been probably the principal sources for the Church's ideas about Judaism.

But what Christians, even those who ought to know better, have too often forgotten is that when Paul said these things, he wasn't writing to Jews or about Jews. He was writing to and about Gentile Christians who had been argued or bullied into thinking that they had to keep the Law: that before they could be Christians, they had to be Jews.

For these Gentile followers of Jesus to submit themselves to the stringent demands of a covenant not their own would indeed have been slavery. But for Jews, living a Torah life is, well, something else—something that I don't really understand. My Orthodox friends approach the Torah, to be sure, with a deep sense of obligation, responsibility, and awe. But they also love it, deeply. They obey it because they love it, and they make time in crowded lives to read books and take classes and look for ways to hew more closely to the Law, to shape their lives more minutely by its precepts, to be more authentically Jewish as they obey more intimately. For observant Jews Torah is not a historical relic nor a dry and oppressive code but a living reality, and to observe it is to enter into a vital, dynamic, all-demanding relationship with God. As Ahuva told me that day outside the shul, the Torah marries Jews to God; it binds them in fidelity to the covenant that makes them who they are.

The second main place where Christians get their image of the Law is straight from the Gospels and particularly from the bitter accusations that Jesus makes when he clashes with the Pharisees, the teachers of the Torah and the forerunners of the rabbis. He calls them hypocrites. He calls them whitewashed tombs. He accuses them of straining at gnats and swallowing camels, of seeking status and power by bullying people about the tiniest details of the Law while themselves sinning gravely against kindness and generosity and humility, against the love of God and neighbor.

Because these are attacks on the keepers of the Law, it is not surprising that many Christians, unfamiliar with Jewish life, come away thinking that obedience to the Law is in itself sterile, superficial, cold. Here again a shallow or uninformed reading is misleading and has been terribly harmful.

Jesus was not criticizing the Torah itself, those who strove to follow it diligently, or those who dutifully led and taught them; it was his Father, after all, who had given the

Torah and ordered his people to obey it. What he was criticizing was hypocrisy, self-righteousness, insincerity, and the manipulation of religious practice and culture in the service of selfish agendas. In doing so Jesus stood in a long tradition of Jews who attacked their fellow Jews every bit as fiercely for the same thing: for failing to recognize that it is not slavish adherence to ritual but the love of God and neighbor that stands at the heart of Torah. The prophets are full of scalding diatribes against superficial piety that masks deep indifference to God himself. In Isaiah God angrily rejects the extravagant religiosity of a violent, greedy, and corrupt society. "Your sacrifices make me sick," he tells them. "Get out of the Temple and leave me alone. Don't bother praying; I'm not listening. Go clean up your act: cease to do evil, learn to do good, seek justice, rescue the oppressed, defend the orphan, plead for the widow. Then we'll talk" (see Isa. 1:12–17). Nor is Jesus alone in calling some Pharisees to account for hypocrisy. The rabbis of the Talmud have a term, *tzevuin*, that means "painted ones"—not unlike Jesus's "whited sepulchers"—and warn against those who ape the Pharisees, who assume an appearance of righteousness out of love for power and prestige rather than love for God.

The Law is from God; it is good. It does not create hypocrisy any more than the doctrine of justification by faith creates complacency or the doctrine of transubstantiation creates superstition. Sinful humans create sins and nourish or justify them with whatever religious materials we have on hand. I'm sure there are plenty of hypocritical Jews—I know there are plenty of complacent and super-stitious Christians—but the Law at the core of Jewish life is not an empty relic but a living mystery.

I won't deny that often, to an outsider like me, it all looks a bit peculiar. Sometimes it looks plain nuts. If my friend Chana is making chicken soup and she's running late and the noodles are boiling over and the toddler is screaming and she accidentally grabs a milk spoon and stirs, she has to stop everything and call Rabbi Goldfarb. He will ask her a string of questions—what the spoon is made of, what temperature everything was, and other things that are halakhically significant for reasons I don't begin to understand—and then he will tell her what to do. As Rabbi Goldfarb is a nice chap, he is on Chana's side and will do his best to find a favorable interpretation of the sit-uation so that she doesn't have to throw out the dinner and start again. However accustomed to Jewish life I become, I am sure there will always be things like this that make me think, *Oh, come on. It's a spoon. You can't be serious.*

My friends cheerfully admit that it is an odd way to live. Once, very hesitantly for fear of giving offense, I asked Ahuva whether maybe, just maybe in rare cases, a high level of observance might possibly become a teeny bit neu-rotic. "Are you *kidding*?" she cackled and launched into a string of disturbing and hilarious anecdotes about weird nuttiness she has come across in the name of Torah obser-vance. But then, anyone who has been a Christian for more than a week and hasn't collected a tidy little store of anecdotes about loony behavior in the name of Christ is either a saint or has absolutely no sense of humor.

I know that many of my non-religious friends and relatives find my faith considerably loopier than I find scrupulous Torah observance. From where they are standing, it's quite bad enough for an intelligent, educated person who has read and traveled and knows what the world is like to believe that there is an all-powerful benign intelligence behind it all. But to believe that the brutal death of a carpenter is, eventually, going to fix everything? And that getting up on Sunday mornings to sit through some preposterous ritual with wine and a wafer is going to help me have a relationship with this carpenter-God? Oh, come on. I can't be serious. But as much as it confounds them, here I am, giving reasonably good signs of being sane. And there are my neighbors, with their milk spoons and meat pots and rabbis, and they look for all the world like warm, cheerful, sensible, witty, perfectly normal people. Go figure.

It is clear to me that their strange vigilance about lightswitches and spoons and the like has brought many of my friends to a faith in, a surrender to, and a relationship with God that is at least as vital, full, and intimate as anything I can claim to have experienced myself. But how it works remains a mystery to me and probably always will. When I try to ask about the connection between observance and spirituality, the conversation invariably founders—

probably because to them the answer to my question is so self-evident, something they take so entirely for granted, that it is hard to put it into words. For an Orthodox Jew, the acts of loving God, being a good person, and faithfully striving to obey all the mitzvahs of the Torah are all one big thing—what Ahuva calls "living a Torah life"—and when I demand that my friends chop a Torah life into artificial chunks and then tell me how they all fit together, they are at first puzzled and eventually, despite their best attempts to hide it, exasperated. My questions must sound arbitrary and pointless to them. They must feel rather like I would if I found myself buttonholed by a curious and persistent Hindu or Taoist who was firmly convinced that the key to understanding Christianity lay in knowing Jesus's shoe size and who resisted all my attempts to steer him onto more interesting topics.

As I cannot persuade my Jewish friends to dissect their religious lives to fit into my Christian categories, I have to make my own guesses. On the one hand, of course, the Law "works" because it is from God. He commanded his people to obey the mitzvahs and promised to reward those who did. Things have changed since then, but God's nature doesn't change, and he will keep his promises. Psalm 1 speaks of the man who keeps aloof from the ways of the wicked and buries himself day and night in the Torah. He will be like a tree by a stream, its roots deep in good soil, growing and flourishing and bringing forth fruit. A human life rooted in Torah will bear fruit the way a tree does—not grudgingly because it has to, nor pridefully to win admiration, but simply because it is its deepest nature to do so. Paul uses the same image of fruitfulness when he writes to the Gentile Christians in Galatia, warning them not to be misled by those who are demanding that they be circumcised. In Christ, he tells them, circumcision and uncircumcision don't matter. Your righteousness is through the Spirit by faith, and if you are led by the Spirit, you are not subject to the Law. If you are led by the Spirit, you will bring forth the fruits of the Spirit. Different covenants, same God, same fruits. Whether you draw your life from lungs filled with the breath of God or from roots deep in the Torah, you will bear fruit, and the fruit is from God.

I love the metaphor of fruit. The image of peaceful and generous abundance is different from the restlessness and tedium and anxiety that too often characterize my spiritual life, but its beauty gives me hope. I want to be like a tree. As part of the process of being received into the Roman Catholic Church—a process based on the practices of the very first Christian centuries—catechumens are asked by the bishop: "What do you seek from God's Church?" My answer was "To live fruitfully," and I have found, in the Church's rich tradition of spiritual disciplines, hints as to how the Torah might "work" in thee lives of my friends.

Mass attendance and Eucharistic adoration and religious images and the rosary and fasts and the liturgical calendar and the daily office can, to be sure, become a servitude motivated only by dull duty or, worse, by lazy superstition. But when they are used rightly, these disciplines do offer peace and abundance by giving us something to do with the parts of our minds and emotions that are normally given to fuss and strain and noise and thus allowing us to be quiet and attend to the ripple of the Spirit deep down in our roots. I imagine that for observant Jews the task of obeying the Law's myriad demands works in much the same way, by keeping their attention focused on God. Six hundred and thirteen mitzvahs demand constant alertness, leaving no space for inattention or sloppiness or indifference.

Of course, I could be quite wrong; maybe the mechanism whereby the deep waters of the Torah are drawn up to swell the fruits of human peace and patience and goodness and joy is quite different. So I will leave the last word on the subject to my husband, a scholar of some very esoteric bits of Jewish and Christian antiquity. "Judaism's *supposed* to be legalistic," he says. "That's how it works. Duh."

9

Darkness and the Triumph of Light

Obedience to the Torah, which energizes every detail of my Jewish friends' lives, does not feel at all to them like sterile slavery to the letter of the Law. But these images of Judaism as servile and sterile, images that are derived from uninformed readings of the Gospels and of Paul, have persisted in the Christian mind for centuries. They are not the only negative images, not the only misunderstandings that have distorted Christians' and others' views of Judaism.

In the Middle Ages there was the blood libel: the rumor, used to incite persecution, about secret Jewish ceremonies that involved the blood of Christian children. There was the notion, stemming from the sociopolitical outworkings of the Roman Catholic Church's ban on usury, of Jews as avaricious and unscrupulous. There are the Protocols of the Elders of Zion: a document first disseminated in nineteenth century Russia by anti-Semitic agents of the czar and purportedly exposing a Jewish plot to attain world domination. Centuries of suspicion and persecution and hatred, fueled by these and other distortions, culminated in the last century with the murder of six million Jews, among them the parents and grandparents of people I know. And it isn't over. There are still people out there who would like to wipe all Jews from the face of the earth.

Lauren Winner writes about her "holocaust fantasies"—about what she would do if

> the rules of exclusion, the rules that say Jews can't do this or that, hold elected office or work in certain professions, those rules start happening, and then violence and other terrible cruelties start happening . . . and spiral and spin . . . and I am somewhere dark and there is mud and there are trains and it is raining.[1]

I think about this too, at one remove. What would I do if the unimaginable happened, and justice and order started disintegrating, and new, sinister powers turned their eyes toward the Jews? Could I be like Corrie ten Boom, Dietrich Bonhoffer, Oskar Schindler, Chiune Sugihara, and many, many others—the Jews call them *hasidei umos haolam*, the righteous among the Gentiles—who risked everything to shelter neighbors and strangers from the grim, terrifying darkness that loomed over them all? Could I risk my own life and the lives of my children for our friends, for justice, for God?

Nothing in my very sheltered life suggests that I have the makings of a hero. So would I be like Peter, who, when the chips were down, chose to abandon his friend to save his own skin? Would I be like the Hutus in Rwanda or the Christian Serbs in Bosnia, who, after living for generations in harmony with their Tutsi or Muslim neighbors, surrendered their souls to a sudden nightmare of hatred and brutality and turned against them? Like the Germans and Poles who stood by and watched what was done to the Jews and did nothing and said nothing?

I don't know what I would do. But I know that even if I failed horribly, if the whole world failed, the Jews would still survive. They will survive whatever fresh terrors the world may yet have in store. The confidence that God will keep his promises has been strengthened rather than undermined, for religious Jews, by the fire they have passed through. To be Jewish today means to be constantly aware and vigilant (to be human today should mean the same), but my friends' vigilance is combined with and deepened by pride, strength, and a commitment to celebration. Jewish festivals, Adina tells me, have a common theme: "They tried to kill us. We won. Let's eat." And although we are in some sense part of the "they"—the Gentile world that has been, for millennia, a constant threat and worse to the Jews—we often get to go along and eat too.

Among the festivals of the Jewish calendar, it is probably Hanukkah, along with Pesach, of which Christians are most aware. Hanukkah commemorates a miracle of light at a dark moment in history. In 165 BC, Israel was under the control of the vast Greek Empire, and the Syrians who controlled the region were aggressively trying to force their subjects to assimilate into the dominant culture. Some Jews were content to adopt Greek language and dress and customs up to a certain point, but there were also stiff-necked conservatives, in the grand tradition of Nehemiah, who angrily resisted all foreign influence. When the Syrian ruler Antiochus Epiphanes ordered the desecration of the Temple, suspicion and resistance erupted into open rebellion, led by a radical known as Judah Maccabeus. (The full account in the book of Maccabbees is a terrific story, stirringly told.) The rebels succeeded in retaking Jerusalem and rededicating the Temple.

As the story goes, they found that almost all the sacred oil used in the Temple menorah had been desecrated. Only one bottle was still sealed, but it contained enough for only one day, and it would take eight days to prepare new oil. The oil in the bottle lasted eight days, and now at Hanukkah Jews light nine-branched menorahs in commemoration of the miracle. Sometimes we get invited to watch. Every member of the family—even the two-year-olds—gets to light their own menorah and say the special blessings. If you have seven or eight kids, then that's a lot of light on the last day when all the candles are lit. There are special foods and presents and games with spinning tops called dreidels, and a good time is had by all.

Hanukkah is fun, but it is not a particularly important part of the Jewish calendar. However, it falls in December, right around the time Christians are decorating trees and wrapping presents; and partly because of this it has become (along with Passover) one of the festivals observed by Jews who don't pay much attention to being Jewish the rest of the year—just as Christmas and Easter bring out a lot of people who don't set foot in a Church the rest of the year. It's ironic, really. Hanukkah celebrates the heroically stubborn refusal of Jews to give way to foreign influence, to budge an inch from their fidelity to their roots or the Law that is their bond to God. But for many Jews who live in a predominately Christian culture, it has come to function as an alternative to Christmas, an excuse to do something with decorations and presents and lights so you can be properly Jewish without cheating the kids.

Or so I'm told. But, of course, this is not true of our neighbors, who, as usual, are blithely indifferent to what Christians are up to. The Orthodox do not suffer from Santa envy; Christmas is "not for Jews," and that's the end of that. It has to be said that the kids do get rather excited about the Christmas tree; let's face it, if you're four years old and your friend's living room suddenly sprouts a ten-foot conifer covered in colored lights and shiny balls, it doesn't matter how Jewish you are—you're going to get excited. And then there's the issue of our manger scene. It's one of those infinitely expandable ones (you start out with Mary and Joseph and baby Jesus and a scattering of angels and shepherds, and then you add a couple of camels and a little drummer boy one year, an elephant and some wise men the next), and our children adore it and play with it constantly. Last year I came into the living room to find Dovid running round and round the coffee table holding baby Jesus and the angel over his yarmulke-clad head, hotly pursued by our Adam and a tyrannosaur who evidently had sinister intentions with regard to the infant Savior. Adam was roaring, "I will eat the baby all up!" And Dovid was yelling, "No, I will save the baby!" I contemplated the scene briefly, then backed into the kitchen and let them get on with it.

In the spring, there's Purim, which also commemorates a triumph of Jewish courage and determination over foreign hostility. The story is set in the Persian Empire. Haman, the wonderfully loathsome villain, is second-in-command to the sleazy, lecherous, drunk King Ahasuerus and has used his influence to plan an attack on the Jews in Persia. One Jew, a minor palace official named Mordecai, has bruised Haman's vast and fragile ego by refusing to grovel to him the way everybody else does, and Haman will not rest until all the Jews in Persia have been slaughtered. The date set for the massacre is drawing near. But unbeknownst to everyone, Ahasuerus's young queen Esther is a Jew—in fact, Mordecai's cousin—and she manages to turn the tables on Haman and save her people. The story, recorded in the book of Esther, is delightful, told with great humor and panache. The author goes to town on the portraits of the nastiness and depravity of the Persian Empire, in which the members of the Jewish community live uneasily, and of the deliciously despicable Haman, whose ego he first inflates then punctures with gleeful wit, leaving Haman utterly humiliated before he is killed.

The story is also rather spicy. Esther is faithful and ingenious and daring, but that is not why she becomes queen. At the start of the story, Ahasuerus dumps his queen in a fit of temper because she coolly declines to be put on display before a palace full of drunk men. He needs to replace her, so beautiful virgins are hauled into the harem and subjected to six months of beauty treatments—surely manicures and eyebrow waxing, and probably lessons on how to address an ambassador and wave graciously and use a fish fork and all the other things queens need to know.

Then they get to meet the king, one at a time. "In the evening she went in; then in the morning she came back" (Esther 2:14). They get to use props. "When the girl went in to the king, she was given whatever she asked for to take with her from the harem to the king's palace," the text says (Esther 2:13). I once asked my class what they thought that might mean, and a bright-eyed freshman, bless her innocent little heart, said, "Something to help the king get to know her? Like maybe a girl might bring a painting she had done or a poem she had written?" Sure, honey. You and I both know that there was a closet in that harem full of the ancient-Persian equivalent of fur-lined handcuffs or hot cinnamon oil (or whatever—I must confess I'm not much of an expert on the twenty-first century versions either). Every girl had a favorite prop and a specialty of her own. But Esther, our heroine, doesn't take anything. And she, alone and unaided by feathers or high-heeled boots, is the one the king chooses to be his queen. Enough said. Fortunately, in addition to being exceptionally talented in the only area that matters to her piggish new husband, Esther has brains and nerve and class, and she uses them to save her people.

The celebration of Purim is rather like Halloween in reverse. Kids, and the grown-ups who are inclined, dress up in costume and go from door to door distributing, rather than demanding, little packets of goodies. Ahuva, who has an offbeat sense of humor and can do anything with a needle, makes costumes for the whole family every year. When I was just getting to know her, she invited me to come and see that year's creations. I knocked on the door in the morning, and Yaakov, who has dark olive skin and big brown eyes with unending eyelashes, opened it. He was wearing a long, narrow white robe and a pointy white hat. He looked at me. I looked at him. He was doubtless thinking, *Why is this strange lady standing at my door and staring at me?* I was thinking, *Oh my! The Ku Klux Klan? I know Ahuva's a bit wacky, but that's really too much.* Before I could collect myself, the rest of the kids came crowding to the door. They were all wearing long, narrow robes and pointy hats. Alisa's were red; Dina's, blue; Simcha's, brown; Yaffa's, yellow. Crayons. *What* a relief. Since then they've been toy soldiers, clowns, and fishermen. But the crayons are still my favorite. One Purim in her wild youth, Ahuva was a pregnant nun.

Then in the evening they drink; if they obey the instructions in the Talmud, they drink until they get Mordecai and Haman muddled up. And the lads go out and raise hell—or they think they do. The spectacle of Orthodox teenagers bent on raising hell is quite hilarious; Orthodox Jews (by comparison to the Catholic kids I teach, or probably in comparison to anyone you care to mention except conceivably the Amish) are very bad indeed at being rowdy, loutish, and antisocial. When I pointed this out to Ahuva, she looked mildly put out and insisted that the teenage boys do get very drunk and behave very badly indeed. She has no clue. None. And that's a good thing.

Sukkot is our family favorite. It is a considerably more important part of the Jewish calendar than Hanukkah and Purim because, unlike them, it is ordained in the Torah and remembers a fundamental part of the story of the covenant: the forty years after the Exodus during which the Jews lived alone in the wilderness with God while the scars of slavery faded and they grew strong enough to take possession of the Promised Land. Leviticus 23:42–43 directs, "You shall live in booths for seven days . . . so that your generations may know that I made the people of Israel live in booths when I brought them out of the land of Egypt; I am the LORD your God."

So late every fall, in remembrance of the forty years in the wilderness, our neighbors' yards sprout little plywood huts with bamboo or branches laid on the top as roofs. Our first time in a sukkah came a few years ago, when the

Levys moved in five doors down one cold, wet October and had to prepare for Sukkot before they were properly unpacked and settled in. Yisroel, who had been told that our house was the place to go for tools and guy things, came over to borrow a spade so he could level a spot for the sukkah in their steep, bumpy, overgrown yard. Glen, spotting an opportunity to be neighborly and get muddy all at once (two of his favorite things), went with him and came back several hours later as muddy as he could have wished, smelling distinctly of whisky, and bearing an invitation for dinner.

The girls were beside themselves with excitement, in large part because they assumed they would get to wear their new party dresses (I don't know where they learned to get so excited about dressing up: not from their mother, that's for sure) and were incensed when I stuffed them into woolly tights, boots, and three layers of sweaters. Their indignation evaporated into delight when we arrived and walked through the living room, through the dining room, through the kitchen, out the back door, through the dark chilly yard, and into the sukkah. It didn't, I imagine, look particularly like the original desert booths, being well furnished with folding chairs, paper chains, and crayon drawings. By Torah law, however, sukkahs cannot be weatherproof—the roof has to be made of natural materials, and you have to be able to see the stars. If the starlight can make it in, so can the rain.

That night it was satisfyingly chilly, but the rain held off just long enough for everyone to do justice to the dinner and for the kids to sing a couple of raucous rounds of "Who Knows One?" a sort of Jewish "Twelve Days of Christmas" except louder and accompanied with energetic gestures and sound effects as it builds on itself from "Who knows one? I know one!" up to "Who knows twelve? I know twelve! Twelve are the tribes of Israel, eleven are the stars in Yosef's dream, ten are the holy commandments," all the way back down to, at the top of your lungs, "One is Hashem! One is Hashem! One is Hashem! In the heavens and the earth." (*Hashem* means "the Name" and is used in everyday conversation to replace *Adonai*, which is used in prayers to replace *YHWH*, the sacred name that God revealed to Moses and that Jews absolutely do not utter, ever. Neither do I, for that matter.)

It would have been hard enough to tear the kids away from the party with Glen's help. This evening it was nearly impossible. By the time it became evident that we had about ten minutes before the children completely fell to pieces, he and the men were surrounded by open books and half-empty glasses, deep into a theological conversation and a bottle, and he really didn't want to leave. I finally pried them all away, and rather than trekking mud into the house for no reason, we walked down the alley to our dark, empty backyard.

By now we more or less take it for granted that we will spend time in a sukkah every year, that someone will bring us little packets of candy at Purim, and that come Hanukkah we will leave our tree for an evening and go watch candles being lit. These celebrations have become part of our year just as Shabbos has become part of our week—a counterpoint playing softly under the melody of the Church's calendar, creating unexpected and poignant harmonies. But the emotional heart of these festivals, celebrations of survival against overwhelming odds, will always remain closed to me. I cannot begin to imagine what it would be like to belong to a people who have been, and still are, the object of vicious hatred. I cannot conceive of what it must be like to learn about the Holocaust for the first time and know that evil was turned against you, your family, and your whole world. It's not something I've discussed with my friends. How exactly are you supposed to start a conversation like that? "Mmm, lovely cookies; you must give me the recipe. And tell me, what's it feel like to have relatives who were experimented on and murdered like animals?" I wish they would tell me about it, because I think I ought to try to understand, even if only a little. But the subject is not mine to raise.

Although Jewish suffering is alien to me, I do feel very comfortable joining in Jewish celebration. Not just because my neighbors are kind and invite us and the food is as good as the company, but because what they are celebrating is God's fidelity to his promises, and our faith rests on that too. Sometimes—if truth be told, quite often—it seems to me preposterous to believe that love will in the end triumph over death, that Christ will return and heal the world.

It doesn't make any sense. But neither does it make any sense that there are menorahs and sukkahs and crowds of noisy kids in costume on my block. It defies all conceivable logic that a tiny nation like Israel should have survived, while civilizations and empires have arisen, triumphed, and crumbled into oblivion. But in defiance of logic, here they are, a blessing to the nations and a blessing to me, and when they invite me to celebrate their crazy victories over history, I'm there with all my heart.

10

God Shows No Partiality

The story in Acts 10–15, from the conversion of Cornelius to the Jerusalem Conference, is probably my very favorite bit of the Bible. All semester I look forward to sharing with my students the intense drama of these chapters. And of all the ways in which my friendship with Jews and my experience of Judaism have influenced me as a Christian, the way I respond to these chapters is possibly the most powerful.

The story begins with Peter and with an odd little incident, which makes little sense at the time but will have unimaginable repercussions later. It's getting on for dinnertime and Peter is hungry. While he's waiting, he goes up to the roof of the house to pray. There he has a vision; animals of all sorts are lowered down from heaven in front of him, and a voice says, "You're hungry? Here, take one of these and make yourself something to eat."

Now, a lot has happened to Peter since, terror stricken, he denied Jesus. He has seen his friend burst the bonds of death, and he has stood up and said so, repeatedly, in front of thousands. He has faced down the Sanhedrin; he has been broken out of prison by an angel; he has been so filled with the power of God that the lame and the sick have crowded around him hoping that his shadow would fall on them. But he doesn't know what to make of this vision. His best guess is that it is a test of his obedience to the Torah. Many in the Jewish hierarchy are increasingly suspicious of those who believe in Jesus; they fear that this wild new movement could undermine the stubborn "neither to the right nor to the left" religious fidelity on which Israel's survival depends. Maybe, Peter thinks, God is suspicious too and wants to know if Peter is getting sloppy. Peter is nettled. "Of course I won't eat that stuff; it's *treif*!" he protests. "Don't you know me better than that, Lord, after all this time?"

I can quite see why he would be put out. I know if I were to offer my neighbors a ham sandwich, they would be offended and hurt. I know their rules; do I think so little of them that I imagine they would brush off one of the central precepts of the Torah for the sake of a snack? It would be rude and disrespectful of me to suggest it.

Is God being rude and disrespectful? He's certainly being persistent—the vision repeats itself, not once but twice, and the voice again urges Peter to kill and eat. It makes me shudder to think of myself repeatedly pushing treif food on Ahuva, Chana, and Adina, pressuring them to break faith with God and their whole people. But this is what God is doing. No wonder Peter is perplexed.

While he is still scratching his head, wondering what on earth Jesus means this time, he is called downstairs to meet visitors, who ask him to accompany them to the house of their master, a Roman centurion who was told in a vision to send for Peter. Peter has to think fast. Of course, a centurion can summon someone like Peter anytime he wants, but Cornelius's servants are being extremely polite—this is very clearly not a summons from a military commander; it is an invitation. Strictly speaking, it is an invitation Peter ought to refuse. He is not supposed to associate with Gentiles any more than he is supposed to eat treif food. Romans were not only the conquerors and enemies of the Jews; they were also pagans, their houses full of graven images of false gods. Jews can't go near that stuff. My friends can't set foot in a Church, and I would no more invite them to come to midnight Mass, or even to our Easter egg hunt, than I would invite them over for cheeseburgers. And now Peter has just had this bizarre vision in which God insisted that he throw Torah and tradition to the wind and make himself a nice cheeseburger. Could it be connected to this invitation? Perhaps it was not a test but a hint: God's way of telling Peter to go with these strangers. If so, it was an obscure hint, but it's all he has to go on, so he sets out with Cornelius's servants.

When he arrives at Cornelius's house, the situation is tense and awkward in the extreme. There is Peter, a fisherman from the provinces, in an elegant villa surrounded by Romans. Cornelius has gathered all his friends, and they are looking at Peter expectantly. Their friend Cornelius had always been a bit, well, odd about religion, and it looks as if he has really lost it this time. *Visions of angels? Is he kidding? What are we doing here? And who is this Jew? He looks like a peasant, for crying out loud.* Worse still is Cornelius himself. He doesn't know what to expect either—who indeed is this Jew whom angels talk about? All he knows is that years of prayer are being answered; he is in such a state of high excitement that when he sees Peter, he throws himself at his feet as if to worship him. Peter, shocked and mortified, has to tell him to get up.

Peter's mind must be working frantically by now. Plunged into a bizarre situation, with nothing to go on but a cryptic clue, he has to make a decision. He clutches at the clue and tells Cornelius, "You know that my people have always regarded yours as profane, unclean. Our laws tell me that I cannot come to you like this. But God has told me not to think of anyone as profane any longer. So here I am. What do you want of me?" When Cornelius tells him his side of the story—his prayers, his vision—Peter says, "Now I truly understand that God shows no partiality."

On the one hand, this is a simple, rather touching exchange between two men from different worlds who find themselves drawn together by a power beyond either of them. It is also a watershed moment in the history of the Church, which up to this day has been composed entirely of Jews who have never considered for a moment that they might ever be anything other than Jews. And for a Jew to say what Peter says—"God has shown me that I must not call anything unclean . . . God shows no partiality"—is astonishing, outrageous. The words of Moses and Nehemiah and the voices of his parents and teachers and friends must have been reverberating in his head as he stood in front of the Roman soldier: "Remember who you are! Remember whose you are! Love the Lord your God and love his Law and meditate on it day and night and never depart from it. He is holy and you must be holy too. Separate yourselves from all that is unholy." And yet, on the strength of a hint tossed to him in a dream, Peter looks Cornelius in the eye and tells him that God makes no difference between them. His daring is breathtaking.

He tells Cornelius and his guests the good news about Jesus. The Holy Spirit descends on them, just as he had descended on Peter and his companions at Pentecost. Now Peter has no more doubts; God is clearly in charge, and Peter has to follow his lead. He baptizes Cornelius and his entire household, and from that moment onwards, the Church is no longer a small group within Judaism but something very different, something that nobody has contemplated before: a family that includes both Jews and Gentiles.

In one afternoon everything has changed. The implications are too huge to contemplate calmly, so the Church does what Peter did —they catch the hint that God tossed them and play it by ear. A pattern quickly establishes itself. When Paul or Barnabas or Luke arrives in a new town to spread the word, they go first to the synagogue and speak to the Jews. Some of them believe and join the disciples, but many, probably most, do not. For generation after generation, the Word of the Lord, backed by bitter experience, has told them to walk in the way that Moses showed them and never to deviate from it, however intense the pressure. It is not surprising that to many Jews, the message about the crucified Messiah and the invitation to be baptized into a new covenant that includes Roman soldiers sounds like a temptation to the kind of infidelity that has nearly destroyed Israel in the past.

There are painful scenes in which Paul and Barnabas are driven from town by hostile congregations of their fellow Jews. They shake the dust of the synagogues off their shoes and strike out into the world of the Gentiles (with their pagan philosophies and their mystery religions and their idols and their treif food and their temple prostitutes and their imperial cults), and they tell them about the Jewish carpenter who died and rose again, and who, it seems, came not only to the Jews but to the whole world to forgive sins. And lots and lots of these Gentiles, these pagans, in Antioch and Iconium and Athens and Corinth and Ephesus, believe and turn from their idols to the one true God and are baptized.

As Gentiles pour into the Church, a rift quickly develops within the leadership. Some Christians, among them many Pharisees, insist that converts be circumcised and taught to keep the Law of Moses. They are horrified by the notion of simply waiving the holy demands of the Torah; if Gentiles are to be Christians, they must become Jews first. It was surely a compelling argument to their fellow Jews, who knew what it was to love Israel and the Torah wholeheartedly. But even more compelling was the evidence of God's activity, the outpouring of the Holy Spirit, the signs and wonders that made no distinction between Jews and Gentiles. The argument of Peter and Paul and the others was very simple: "God is at work. We need to get out of his way."

The debate between the two sides becomes bitter, and a meeting is called in Jerusalem to talk the problem through and to make some serious decisions about what exactly to do about this new breed of Spirit-filled, Messiah-worshipping Gentiles. The decision comes down to James, the leader of the Jerusalem Church. He listens to both sides and agrees, to a limited degree, with the conservative insistence that certain things are nonnegotiable. Gentiles who turn to Jesus, he says, and seek baptism for the forgiveness of sins must utterly renounce idolatry: no household shrines, no muttered prayers, nothing that reminds them of their old gods. They must not eat meat with blood. And they must turn from the license of their pagan pasts and adopt the high standards of sexual purity that have set the Jews apart from their neighbors. Of the 613 mitzvahs of the Torah, these three remain. As regards the other 610, James agrees with Paul's party that "we should not trouble those Gentiles who are turning to God" (Acts 15:19). It is a momentous decision, and with it the future relations of Christianity and Judaism are sealed. It is inevitable that Christianity is going to pull away from Judaism, appeal less and less to Jews in the grand tradition of Nehemiah, and forge a new path.

The conservative, or "Judaizing," party does not give up without a fight. They send out missionaries of their own, trying to persuade Gentile converts to be circumcised. Paul fights back; he builds the foundations of Christian theology on the claim that the salvation won by Jesus is received by faith. He says that Gentile Christians have been adopted into the family God began with the election of Abraham, and that Abraham's righteousness was by faith. He says that circumcision is a sign of God's covenant, not a condition. He also says, passionately, that it breaks his heart to watch Judaism and Christianity going in separate directions; that at times it is so painful to him he is almost ready to abandon his own salvation, if his salvation requires him to abandon his people; and that he doesn't understand why God has let this happen but knows God will keep his promises.

This story, the story of how Christianity and Judaism came to be two separate religions, has been transformed for me since I have lived in close proximity to Judaism. Before I came here, I respected Judaism as a noble and ancient tradition, the bedrock of my own, but had no sense of how one might love it as a vibrant, living reality. Now that I do, my response to this story is intense and full of conflict. Of course, I still read it as a Christian; and of course, it is thrilling. On the roof in Joppa, God shows an uncomprehending Peter that he meant what he said when he told Abraham that through him all the nations of the world would be blessed. In Cornelius's villa the knowledge of the Lord and the message about Jesus and the forgiveness of sins are thrown open to the whole world. At the Jerusalem Conference, the Church puts its trust in God, reaches out to people it had been taught to avoid, and steps into a future it could not imagine or comprehend. I love and admire Peter and Paul and James for their fearless, selfless, openhearted trust. But I have also come to appreciate the determination and fidelity of the Jews who held out, disputed with Paul and Barnabas, and rejected their message of a new covenant—they are the ancestors of my neighbors, the people who have kept Judaism alive. I have learned to sympathize also with the conservative party at the Jerusalem Conference. I used to think of them as grouchy, unimaginative sticks-in-the-mud, but now I see them as motivated by the deep love for Torah that characterizes the lives of my friends. I can understand their horror at the idea that the Gentiles should be accepted as worshipers of God without being required to keep God's holy Law in its entirety. And I can feel, acutely, Paul's anguish as he watches Israel and the Church inexorably pull apart, forget their deep kinship, and prepare to forge separate paths through history. I know what that history is going to be like.

It is God's story, and it is not for me to wish it otherwise. But I am torn in all directions when I read these chapters. It is not a shallow, triumphalistic account of "how we shook off the shackles of tradition," but a tense story of faithful Jews struggling to understand God's will and to make a decision that will have huge implications for all of God's people. The stakes are high, and there is tragedy among the triumph. The world was won for Christ, but the cost was very high. The daring decisions of the story's heroes, Peter and James and Paul, are noble in part because, as these men steered the fledgling Church into uncharted waters, they must have known how much would be lost.

11

Us and Them

So here we are, cheek by jowl with the life that we might have been leading had Peter and James sided with the conservatives in Jerusalem and decided that Christians did, indeed, need to be Jews first. My husband has his own yarmulke for those occasions when one needs a yarmulke. Our kids draw stars with six rather than five points and tell us jokes with Hebrew punch lines. If we get invited to a shalom zachor, we know, without being told, the day and time we should show up. We know all kinds of random halakhic trivia: Jews eat cheese on Shavuos and fruit on *Tu B'Shevat*, they don't listen to music during *Tisha b'Av*, and they throw bits of bread into running water at Rosh Hashanah.

It's lots of fun, but there have been some excruciating moments. Once, on vacation, we found ourselves in a museum elevator with an Orthodox family. Fearing what might happen, I jabbered merrily about the dinosaurs but to no avail—Catherine and Elisabeth chirped in unison

"Oh, hello! You're Jews!" The doors opened before I had time to stammer out an explanation. Then there was the time at the park when Catherine was playing with a little boy while I chatted to his very pleasant father. Catherine's little friend mentioned, apropos of I can't remember what, that he was Jewish, whereupon Catherine looked him up and down—no yarmulke, no tzitzis—and said coolly, "Hmm, you must be one of those Jews who don't know their mitzvahs."

Sometimes, like Catherine, I start to feel smugly that I'm an insider, that I "get it," that I really understand Orthodox life. Of course, I don't: far from it. When we're invited to an "event"—a party, a bris, somewhere there is a large group— and I am on the fringes of conversations that are not organized around including me and making allowances for my ignorance, I realize how weirdly, bewilderingly different than our world is the world my friends inhabit. Like Catherine, I've made more than my fair share of klutzy faux pas. In the shul just the other week, at the end of a bris, I actually began to genuflect on my way out of the sanctuary: religious event, ceremonial space, force of habit. I don't *think* anybody noticed. At the dinner afterwards I found myself at a table with strangers—the children had vanished with their friends, and Glen, of course, resplendent in his yarmulke, was sitting with the men on the other side of the room. A table full of strangers makes me a little shy—it probably makes most everybody a little shy—so I fell back on the usual vocabulary of female small talk: "How many children do you have?" and so on. After I had asked this for the third time and received an odd answer, the woman beside me gently explained that you're not supposed to ask "how many" questions about people. Next time I'll know. But for every mitzvah, and every halakhic gloss on a mitzvah, and every custom, tradition, legend, or belief that I stumble across, there are hundreds, probably thousands, I have no idea about.

At parties, when not actively making a fool of myself, I am interrupting. All conversations, whatever the topic, switch back and forth between English and Hebrew and Yiddish; there is no aspect of life—absolutely none—that is not touched by Torah and sprinkled with foreign words. I have become quite shameless about butting in: "Hey, hang on! So ten seconds ago we were talking about the sale at Penney's and now we're talking Hebrew. What is going on, and what is Jewish about Penney's?" And they'll grin and explain that there is a mitzvah about the kinds of fibers that can and can't be mixed in the same garment, and that if you buy something made of wool, before you can wear it you have to send it for testing to make sure there is no linen anywhere in it. That's what is Jewish about Penney's.

There's nothing unusual about my making a fool of myself. I don't need to go to a bris for that; I can do it anywhere. But what is really quite unusual is for a Catholic to be even very partially at home in the world of ultra-Orthodox Judaism. It is, by and large, a world that keeps to itself. There are any number of reasons for this: theological—God commanded the Jews to keep themselves apart from the nations; historical—they've been brutalized for centuries; practical—because once you start inviting Gentiles to your parties, you can't get through half a sentence without having to stop and launch into complicated explanations of something or other.

Several factors have made our unusual situation possible. First, this isn't a big city. Many of the Jewish families are transplants from New York (you can buy a six-bedroom house with a garden here for the cost of a closet in Brooklyn, which is useful if you have eight children), and they come here knowing that they will be mingling with a more diverse world. The community is thriving and growing, but it is too small—about sixty or seventy families—to be self-contained like the big Hasidic neighborhoods in New York, where shop signs are in Yiddish and a woman with her hair uncovered would stand out as much as a woman walking down the street in her underwear.

Second, thanks to our education and profession, when we moved into the neighborhood we had a knowledge of Scripture, theology, and history well above the average, as well as a basic familiarity with the notion of strict Jewish observance. This meant that we could talk to our neighbors without their having to explain themselves from the ground up. I knew what *Torah* meant, and *kosher* and *halakha* and *mitzvah* and *minyan*, and why everyone walked down the street in their best clothes at dusk on Friday. The first time Yaffa asked her mum if she could come and play at our house, I knew enough to say, "Don't worry, I won't let her eat anything. Is tap water okay? Paper cup? Got it." It only took one brief moment of embarrassment for me to learn not to attempt to shake hands with an Orthodox man. I ask an awful lot of questions, but they are usually reasonably well-informed questions, not the sort to elicit a "Gosh . . . er . . . I don't really know where to begin . . . You see, we're Jewish, and we have a lot of rules . . ." response. I'm sure our ignorance, coupled with our curiosity, is tedious at times, but it was never colossal enough to make it simply too much effort for our neighbors to talk to us about anything other than the weather.

Third, we got lucky with our neighbors. All the Orthodox we have met have been pleasant and friendly and are at least as happy to pass the time of day with us as the neighborhood Catholics and Pentecostals and secular humanists are, but we probably never would have got beyond passing the time of day were it not that, about a year after we moved in, the Gindoffs bought the house four doors down. We have all kinds of things in common: their younger children are the same ages as ours and have the same soft hearts and quirky, eccentric little minds; their house, like ours, is cheerfully chaotic, reassuringly messy, and perpetually cluttered with books; we all, adults included, share a geeky obsession with Harry Potter and Star Wars; we can all talk the hind leg off a donkey. We quickly became friends. Our kids are inseparable. Ahuva visits my classes to talk about living a Torah life; Zevi drops round regularly to talk politics and check that Glen's fifteen-year-old single-malt scotch is still kosher. They find it entertaining to see themselves through our eyes: "Hey, Maria, guess what? If you slaughter a cow then find out it had milk in its udders, the milk counts as meat . . . Cool, huh? Not that I've ever heard of it happening—I mean, you don't kill dairy cows for meat, do you? But still, you never know." They also know absolutely everybody—she is the only kosher caterer in town, and he is the chair of B'nai B'rith—and are widely acknowledged to be probably the nicest people on the planet. "Friends of the Gindoffs" is an instant password to a welcome in situations in which non-Jews do not normally find themselves.

In the main, our experiences here have been important personally, for reasons only indirectly connected with religion. This is a really wonderful neighborhood in which to raise a family. It's not fancy by any means—there's a lot of peeling paint and cars with missing hubcaps and broken toys on porches—but it's a real community. People know each other and look out for each other. Plus there are loads of nice kids around; kids who, like ours, inhabit a world without video games or cable television, kids who can be relied on never to set undesirable examples with regard to skimpy T-shirts or permissive curfews. I doubt the same could be said for many ritzy, SUV-lined suburbs in America today.

We have also learned some things about being friends with people who are different from ourselves. Learning these things is not only fun and interesting; it also might be quite important in a small way. The big world outside our happily diverse little neighborhood is shrinking rapidly, and we—the human family, long-lost cousins all—are bumping up against and getting entangled with people who are very different from ourselves. It is, by and large, a difficult business to live in close proximity with people who are different: always has been, always will be. But we have to learn to do it, or we may not make it into the next century. We cannot afford to retreat into bigotry and suspicion and triumphalism. On the other hand, we can't afford simply to jettison whatever convictions and commitments might clash with the convictions and commitments of others, because when the going gets tough—and it will—we're going to need our convictions and commitments.

Most of what enables our Orthodox friends and us to get on smoothly around our differences is just a matter of common courtesy and common sense. It's common courtesy to shut up and listen while other people tell you who they are, rather than deciding that you know already. It's common sense that sometimes being around people who see things very differently can be awkward and that you need to tolerate a bit of awkwardness and not take yourself too seriously. We feel comfortable around the very different world our neighbors inhabit because nobody pretends that the worlds aren't different. The boundaries between us and our Orthodox neighbors are unequivocally clear, and nobody tries to hide them or gloss over them. Nobody acts as if they are silly or embarrassing or as if they are superficial or don't really matter. They do matter, and everybody knows it. We know they think our food is gross. They know we think some of the mitzvahs are weird and some of their traditions a bit nutty. We know that a marriage between one of their children and one of ours would constitute a major family crisis for them. They know that we wouldn't be too keen on it either. We can all make jokes about it.

Of course, I know that we are merely dipping our toes in the shallows of diversity. While our Orthodox neighbors are really quite different in many ways, we are very similar in many, many others. We're all middle-class urban Americans with minivans and snow shovels and cell phones and library cards and jobs. It would be absurd to suggest that our experience here offers an easy solution to the challenges of our moment in history. There are terrible injustices and cruelties in the world, and terrible anger and pain that are not going to be healed by the courtesy and common sense and humor that make our relationships here work. If we—the human family—are to learn to live in peace, we will need love (which drives out fear) and humility (which dissolves pride). But love and humility are deep mysteries; they demand that we give ourselves up, and that is a terrifying prospect. Courtesy and common sense and humor are within reach of more of us and are probably not a bad place to start.

Ironically, it may actually be the differences between

ourselves and our Orthodox friends that make it possible for us to be friends in the first place. If they were Christians or we were Jews, I don't think the friendship would work. If the Gindoffs, say, were Christians, they would still be kind, warm, friendly people; but I probably wouldn't notice, because I would be driven beside myself with frustration by some things about them: a conviction that the universe is about 5,700 years old; a fascination with colorfully detailed apocalyptic scenarios; a cheerful assumption that they share with Abraham and Solomon and Habakkuk and Paul a single coherent philosophy called a "biblical worldview."

I expect it would work the other way too. If we were the sort of Jews that we are Christians, we would keep kosher at home but not bother about it too much when eating out; we would make a sincere attempt to make Shabbos a special day but wouldn't think twice about driving to the store if we were out of milk; we would prefer our kids to marry Jews but would suck it up and go to our grandchildren's baptisms if that's the way things worked out. Our neighbors don't have much patience with that sort of Judaism.

I imagine that if we belonged to the same religion, we would probably keep each other at a polite but faintly disdainful distance. But as their religion is not our business and our religion is not theirs, our friendships are not derailed by our cherished prejudices and irritations and opinions. It does make one wonder why we so easily allow our prejudices and irritations and opinions to make such a splintered mess of the Church, of Christ's body, when he told us so clearly not to. But that's a whole other issue.

For Glen and me, the experience of crossing in friendship boundaries that are not usually crossed has been a fascinating and enlightening adventure. For our children, it is simply the way life is. That some people are Christians and believe in Jesus and some are Jews and don't, and that Christians and Jews do things differently, is something they absorbed along with the fact that if they want ice cream, they have to say please. They know, without having to think about it, which coloring books, which movies, and even which episodes of *VeggieTales* are okay when their friends are round on a rainy afternoon. They don't think it at all odd that they can have lunch at Yitzy's house but Yitzy can't even have an apple out of our fruit bowl. Navigating smoothly around those differences, without letting them interfere with the serious business of fun, is second nature to them:

"We've got to have lunch now, so you'd better go home, but can we come to yours after?"

"Leave Avi's tzitzis *alone*, Adam. I know they're nice, but you're Catholic, and you can't have them."

"It's time for me to go for my bath. I'll try to come back later, but I'll have my Shabbos clothes on, so we'll have to play inside."

"I'd better be Piglet, because he's not kosher. Do you want to be Tigger or Pooh?"

It will get more complicated as they get older, as the

differences between their lives become more apparent and friendships between boys and girls start to come under closer parental scrutiny. I confidently anticipate broken hearts that will take, oh, days to mend. But however complex the questions and answers will become, they will arise among friends for whom the differences between Jewish and Christian worlds cause less friction than burning questions about who pushed whom first, or whose turn it is for the sparkly shoes or the green light saber. As an elementary preparation for civilized participation in the global village, it's hard to beat.

12

One Is Hashem

It's been six years now since I was in Jerusalem when Shabbos arrived. There's been a lot of gefilte fish and knishes and kosher wine in those years; chilly dinners in sukkahs and giggly, blurry drinks at Purim. Above all there have been countless hours kibitzing on doorsteps and pestering my immensely patient neighbors with endless questions about the ritual of the mikveh and kabbalah and why you have to eat cheese on Shavuos. But my Jewish friends never ask me, "So how does this Trinity idea work?" or "Do you speak English in Church?" or "What's the deal with the pope and contraception anyway?" or expressed any curiosity about what we believe or do as Christians.

Nor have I ever raised the subject. When I was new to the neighborhood, I mentioned to a Jewish colleague that I was getting to know some of my Orthodox neighbors, and he told me that I should never talk about religion. Anything that could possibly be interpreted as an attempt at proselytism would bring budding friendships to a screeching halt. There are strong reasons for this: both historical reasons—the forced conversion of Jews under the Spanish Inquisition, the medieval practice of compelling rabbis to participate in humiliating and heavily rigged public debates with Christian theologians—and more recent reasons. The enemies of the Jews (and there have been many) have been not only those like Haman and Hitler who sought their extermination, but also those like Nebuchadnezzar and Antiochus Epiphanes who tried to force them to assimilate, to melt into history, to worship the gods of the nations, to forget their own story, and to be lost. It made sense, and I took his advice.

Of course, by now our neighborhood friendships are well established. Everybody who knows us knows we are Christians—we certainly don't hide it—and nobody is going to think I'm anti-Semitic if I venture an explanation of what happens at Mass or what Paul says about Abraham or try to make it clear that, despite appearances, Christians really do believe in only one God. Glen and Zevi occasionally pull out the Talmud and the New Testament and compare passages. But, by and large, they don't ask and we don't tell.

If I did—if I pointed out to my friends all the ways in which the coming of Jesus fulfills the prophecies of the Scriptures that we share, if I read them Isaiah on the Suffering Servant and then Mark's account of the Passion, if I showed them the first few chapters of Matthew, or Peter's sermon on Pentecost, or (if I were feeling particularly pushy) Stephen's speech before the Sanhedrin—I imagine they would coolly turn to Isaiah 2, "They shall beat their swords into plowshares, and their spears into pruning hooks; nation shall not lift up sword against nation, neither shall they learn war any more" (v. 4b), or Isaiah 11, where it says that when the new David, the shoot from the stump of Jesse, comes, he will take the side of the meek of the earth and put an end to the wickedness of the wicked, and wolves and lambs and babies and snakes will live in peace in a world without hurt or destruction. They would say, "*This* is what will happen when Moshiach comes. Look around you. Does this honestly look like the history of the last couple of thousand years from where you're standing? Because, let me tell you, from where we're standing, it really, really doesn't." And I imagine that they would be singularly unimpressed by my arguments about the Second Coming and the intricacies of Christian eschatology and the hope that the Church has been holding aloft since Paul wrote to reassure the Thessalonians that Christ would return as he had promised, although no one knew the day or the hour.

That's what I imagine would happen if we had the conversation. I wish we could. There's nothing I like better than a heated discussion about religion with good friends. We have an ardently agnostic colleague who finds religion absurd but fascinating, and who shares our taste for staying up late, arguing, and brandishing colorful and good-humored insults. We have spent many a night in ferocious debate with him, having a grand old time and getting absolutely nowhere before realizing that the bottle is empty and the children will wake up in about four hours. All things being equal, we could do the same with our Orthodox friends, cheerfully slinging Bible verses back and forth. "Aha! But in 1 Peter it says . . . Whaddya say to *that*, then?" But all things aren't equal, and I very much doubt that we ever will.

Our children know that they are not to say too much about Jesus and Church to their Jewish friends. Of course, it is no secret that we are different from them: our food is treif, for a start, and there are rosaries and icons and crosses around rather than mezuzahs, not to mention that splendid sparkly tree we get around Hanukkah, with the baby and the angels, and all the camels. But I discourage them from getting into it too much. I am tickled pink if my children teach me bits of Yiddish or the proper berakha to say before eating fruit or after using the bathroom, but I don't think Ahuva would feel the same if Yaffa were to teach her the Our Father or sing "Jesus Loves Me" at bedtime.

Our children have as good an understanding of the situation as anybody could at their age; they can explain that Jews are different from Christians because they knew God before anybody else did and he gave them special rules. The mitzvahs are how they are friends with God, and now Jesus is how we and everybody else can be his friends. "But," they ask quite reasonably, "if we are all God's friends, and if

Jesus really is God's Son, then why can't we make them Christmas cards, and why can't we invite them to baptisms or first communions or Easter egg hunts?"

"Well," we tell them, "they would think it was rude."

"But why would they think it was rude? *We* think it's a big treat to go over for Sukkot or Purim, and *we* don't think it's rude when they talk about mitzvahs or make us Hanukkah cards. We like it. Besides, Jesus was Jewish, so why can't we tell them about him?"

To this we answer that people who said they were Christians used to be horrible to Jews, and lots of Jews are still really sad about it. God's really sad about it too, we say, and the best thing we can do for now is just be good friends and let him take care of everybody and fix the bad stuff, because he's the only one who understands how. It's not sophisticated, I know, and there are holes in it. But after all, we're talking about seven-year-olds here, and for the moment, it will do.

I am largely in the dark on a subject I am intensely curious about: what my Orthodox friends know and understand and think about Christianity and what they say to their children about us. If I had to hazard a guess, I'd imagine they say what I'd say to my children if the nice family down the block were Mormons. I'd say, "They're great kids, and I'm really glad you're friends. You've probably noticed that they go to kind of a funny Church and they have some odd ideas about God. If they tell you stories about an angel called Moroni or somebody called Joseph

Smith and some tablets, you can just tell them that we're Catholic and we don't believe in that. Don't argue with them; it's really important to them and we don't want to hurt their feelings, but just between us, it's pretty silly."

That's just a guess. Maybe they say nothing of the sort. But Christians do, in one sense, stand in the same relation to Jews as Mormons or Jehovah's Witnesses stand in relation to traditional Christianity. From the point of view of the older religion, in each case, the younger looks like a strange twist that, for some reason, seized the imagination of a group of followers, took on a life of its own, and became a whole new religion, while claiming to be the legitimate fulfillment of the parent religion. Mormons think of themselves as Christians, but most Christians don't feel obliged to take Mormonism particularly seriously. In the same way, Christians can never forget or turn their backs on Judaism; in fact, we call the Church "the new Israel." But at this point in history it would be foolish to expect Jews to take seriously our claim to be children of Abraham just like them. So I don't. (Of course, the analogy is thrown off by the fact that Mormons don't outnumber Christians by more than a hundred to one. If they did, I am sure I would not take kindly to their knocking on the door trying to convert the few of us still stubbornly keeping the faith. As it is, I always invite them in.)

There are many Christians, I know, who would find it sad or scandalous (or worse) that I do not talk about the gospel with my Jewish friends, who would say that in failing to proclaim to them the message about Christ, I show myself to be a friend neither to them nor to him. There is an interesting argument to be had there, for sure. But I am not going to have it here, nor am I going to attempt to justify my own practice, except to say more or less what I say to my children: that both the history and the theology of relations between Jews and Christians are complicated and often painful, and that the best thing we can do for now is just be good friends and let God take care of everybody and fix the bad stuff, because he's the only one who understands how. That may sound dreadfully lazy—especially coming from a theologian, whose job it is to think about these things. I have read and reread Romans, where Paul wrestles with these questions, and every time I hear him saying something different. And now the story is two thousand years longer and a whole lot more complicated, and even to the extent that I can and should try to follow Paul in wrestling with the great cosmic story of God and Christ and the Jews, the relationship between God and Christ and our Jewish friends is, I think, not something I ought to be meddling in. We try to live our lives as faithful Christians: to walk in the light of Christ. What, if anything, our neighbors make of it is their business and God's, not ours.

It would be discourteous, and possibly hurtful, of me to disregard our neighbors' desire not be drawn into religious debate. It would also be, I feel, ungrateful. And I have a lot for which to be grateful. By coming, through great trial, to know the one God and to worship him alone by receiving the Torah, by obeying the laws he gave them, the Jews prepared for God the place where he would dwell among us, where he would become flesh, and where he would enter our world to seek and find those who did not know him. The Jews gave Christ to the world. And, as I have come to understand over the last six years, they continue to give Christ to the world. It seems to me quite impossible that the Church should live its life, baptize, and break bread, and that believers should be filled with the Spirit, in a world in which there were no Jews keeping kosher, welcoming Shabbos, and learning Torah. I don't understand it, but there it is. There could be no Church in a world that had utterly forgotten the Torah.

This is not just a historical or theological statement, but a personal one. My neighbors have given me Christ in myriad ways. My briskly modern and pragmatic approach to daily life has been challenged by seeing how food and time and clothing and everything are commandeered in my neighbors' lives by the command to be holy. I believe, with Paul and the Church, that God saves us in Christ by faith, but I have come to see that there is something salvific about the Law too. The liturgical life of the Church is enriched when it is lived shoulder-to-shoulder with the Jewish year. Sunday, the day of the Resurrection, dawns with new meaning when it follows the sacred hush of Shabbos. The drama of the Eucharist is deepened by the counterpoint of the Seder. Even Christmas has added poignancy from coming in the wake of Hanukkah; the powers of darkness have not overcome the Jews, and they will not overcome the light of the star over the stable. My relation to the Bible has been transformed, and my understanding of it has been deepened by a glimpse, however distant, into the lives of the people who wrote it. The Old Testament is more exciting now that I see the Torah lived all around me, and the New Testament is more dramatic now that I understand more clearly the wrenching decisions that confronted Peter and Paul as they brought word of Messiah and Spirit into an alien world.

Every semester, when I read through the Bible with my students, I find myself caught up in the drama and catch myself taking the side of the conservatives at the Jerusalem Conference, wanting to draw the Gentiles into the world of Torah. I find the lives of my neighbors fascinating and beguiling, and there are moments when I am half a Judaizer myself and catch myself idly musing that wouldn't it maybe be a nice way of connecting with the whole history of our faith if we did something with candles on Friday evenings or kept, well, just a *very* little bit kosher, like, say, no bacon cheeseburgers? I was, I must admit, even a little drawn to the nutty "Yeshua is Moshiach!" of Christians-turned-Jews-turned-Christians in Jerusalem. But every semester, Paul's exclamation, "You foolish Galatians! Who has bewitched you?" (Gal. 3:1) calls me back to reality; that question was settled two thousand years ago. In the eyes of the world, and for all practical purposes, Judaism and Christianity are separate religions now; and we have all but forgotten that at the birth of the Church, a family was ripped apart. It is hard for us to relate to Paul's anguish at the unavoidable parting of the ways.

But now I can, just a little. Paul said that the Church is a new branch grafted into the older vine of Israel, that by faith in Christ the Gentiles are adopted and made children of Abraham and of God. Before I came to live in this neighborhood, I understood the theological import of the metaphor, but I didn't respond emotionally to hearing that I had been adopted into a family I had never met. Now that I have met them, two thousand years after Paul lamented over them, I find that the metaphor of adoption speaks to me from a different angle. I sometimes feel as if I had been adopted at birth into a good and loving family, the only family I have ever had or will ever think of as mine. But now, as an adult, I have accidentally stumbled across my biological family and have become, rather hesitantly, friends with them: borrowing their books, leafing through their photo albums, going shopping with my half sisters. It has helped me to understand things about myself that never quite made sense before—my passion for spicy food and bad science fiction, my inability to be on time for anything, ever. All of a sudden these things have a context, and I know what they're about. It's fascinating, but it does hurt a little bit. I wish I could belong to both families at once—keep Mom and Dad and the kid brother I grew up squabbling with, and somehow be part of this new (or is it old?) family too. And it makes me sad that, although they are all being awfully nice to each other, they are different families and always will be; and there's nothing I can do about it.

But this state of affairs is temporary. Paul says that now we see in a glass, darkly, but the day will come when we will see face-to-face and know God as he know us. Ahuva puts it rather differently; she says, "When Moshiach comes, we'll just ask him, 'So then, have you been here before, or is this your first visit?'" Until then, we will have to go on wondering why God has done things this way.

Why the whole of Israel did not turn to Jesus is a mystery to the writers of the New Testament and, therefore, remains a mystery to Christian theology. To the Church's first leaders, devoted Jews, it was a tragic, frustrating mystery. To Paul, who loved his people and loved Torah, it was heartbreaking. He knew that God was in control and that his promises to Israel were eternal and would be honored. But despite his trust in God's faithfulness, the division between the Jews who followed him out of the synagogues and those who remained was, for him, an open and agonizing wound. I have come to love Judaism from the outside and can imagine what it must be to love it as one's own and yet to see oneself parted from it. I have been enriched as a Christian by being able to understand, just a little, Paul's pain.

At Mass, after the consecration prayer, with the presence of Christ among us, the priest says, "Let us proclaim the mystery of faith." I'm always relieved that he calls it a mystery, because most of the time I am completely mystified by it. We respond, "Christ has died; Christ is risen; Christ will come again." Mystified as I am, I'll go on proclaiming that Christ *will* come again. And when he comes, my neighbors will greet him as their own. Not "Oops! So the Christians were right after all!" but "So here you are, finally! Baruch Hashem! What took you so long?"

At that moment, the glass in which we see darkly will melt into uncreated light, the veil will fall from our eyes, and we will all see him—Hashem, the Christ, the One—face-to-face and call him and each other by our true names.

Glossary

Some terms will probably require explanation. Like everything else in this book, I have learned these not from scholarly sources but from conversation with my neighbors. Some of the terms, like berakha are Hebrew and some, like Shabbos or shul are Yiddish—the the blend of Hebrew, German and Polish that was the lingua franca of Eastern European Jews for centuries. Because the roots are all Hebrew, there is some variation in spelling; the ones I use are, again, approved by a neighbor. In the pronunciation guide, "kh" stands for a rough guttural throaty sound that I still can't do properly, although my children can.

(A note on plurals: strictly speaking, the plural of mitzvah is mitzvot, and of berakha is berakhot. But my neighbors say "mitzvahs" and "berakhas," so that is what I have done.)

Adonai (AH-doh-nye), Hebrew for "God," used in prayer

Aron Kodesh (ERR-on KO-desh), a cabinet in the synagogue that holds the Torah scrolls

baal teshuvah (bahl ti-SHOO-vah) literally "master of repentance"—a Jew who is not raised Orthodox but voluntarily takes on Orthodox observance

bar mitzvah (bar MITS-veh), a celebration on a Hebrew boy's thirteenth birthday, of his completing his Jewish study

Baruch Hashem (bar-OOKH ha-SHEM), "Thank God"—a frequent expression, as in, "How are you?" "Baruch Hashem, I'm well."

berakha (BRA-khah), a blessing or benediction

B'nai B'rith (beh-nay BRITH), an international Jewish organization promoting the betterment of Jews and the public at large through culture, society, and education

bris *pl.* **brissim** (briss), the celebration upon the circumcision of a male child eight days old

Chumash (KHOO-mash), the Pentateuch

chuppah (KHOO-puh), a canopy under which the Jewish marriage ceremony is performed

dreidel (DRAY-dl), a four-sided top used in children's games during Hanukkah

gefilte fish (guh-FILL-teh fish), freshwater fish, blended with eggs, matzoh meal, and seasoning, shaped into balls and simmered in vegetable broth, often served chilled

halakha (hall-LAH-khuh), the entire body of Jewish law and tradition, including Torah, Talmud, and oral law; **halakhic** *adj.*

Hanukkah (KHA-neh-kuh), an eight-day festival celebrating the Maccabean victory over the Syrians

Hashem (ha-SHEM), "the Name"—how Orthodox Jews refer to God in conversation

hashkafa (hash-KAH-fah), Jewish ethics or worldview

Glossary

hasidei umos haolam (hah-SID-ay OO-mes hah-OH-lum), "the righteous among the nations"; virtuous Gentiles)

kabbalah (kuh-BAA-luh), the tradition of Jewish mysticism

kashruth (KASH-root), the body of Jewish dietary law

kibitz (KIB-its), to joke, wisecrack, or offer advice

knish (knish), a fried roll of dough with filling

kosher (KO-shur), fit to be eaten according to Jewish dietary law

loshon (LOW-shen), proper speech

matzoh ball (MAT-seh ball), a dumpling made from matzoh meal, usually served in soup

menorah (me-NOR-uh), a candelabra with nine branches for use during Hanukkah

mezuzah (meh-ZOO-zuh), a parchment scroll on which Deuteronomy 6:4-9 and 11:13-21 are inscribed on one side and the word *Shaddai* on the other, kept in a small tube on the doorpost of Jewish homes

mikveh (MEHK-vah), a ritual bath Orthodox Jews are required to take on certain occasions, as before Shabbos and after each menstrual period

minyan (MIN-yan), the number of people required by Jewish law to be present to conduct a religious service (typically a minimum of ten Jewish males over thirteen years old)

mitzvah (MITS-vah), six hundred thirteen rules in the Bible and Talmud

Moshiach (ma-SHEE-akh), Messiah

Novi (NUII-vee), the Prophets

Pentateuch (PEN-tuh-too k), the first five books of the Old Testament

Pesach (PAY-sahk), Passover

Purim (POOR-im), a festival celebrating the deliverance of the Jews from destruction in Persia

Rosh Hashanah (rosh ha-SHAH-nuh), a high holy day that marks the beginning of the Jewish New Year

Seder (SAY-duhr), the ceremonial dinner that commemorates the Jewish exodus from Egypt

Shabbos (SHA-bus), Hebrew term for "Sabbath"

Shabbos goy (SHA-bus goy), a gentile who performs tasks for Jews on Sabbath that are forbidden by Jewish law

shalom zachor (SHU-lem ZU-kher), a party on the first Friday evening of a baby boy's life

Shavuos (shah-VOO-os), a festival commemorating God's giving the Ten Commandments to Moses

shomrei negiyah (SHOME-ray neg-EE-yuh), to refrain from physical contact before marriage

shomrei yichud (SHOME-ray YI-khud), prohibition on males and females being alone together

shul (shool), Yiddish term for synagogue

Sukkot (soo-KOT), festival commemorating the harvest and period the Jews wandered in the wilderness

sukkah (SOO-kah), a booth or hut built with branches

Talmud (TAL-mood), collection of Jewish law

Tisha b'Av (TAY-shah beh-AV), a fast observed in memory of the destruction of the temples

Torah (TOR-uh), both the Pentateuch and the entire body of Jewish law

treif (trayf), non-kosher food, literally "torn"

Glossary

Tu B'Shevat (too bi-sheh-VAT), the fifteenth day of Shevat, observed as a new year for trees

tzevuin (ze-VOO-in), "painted" or "shady"

tzitzis (tse-tset), the fringes or tassels worn at the corners of outer garments

tznius (ZNEE-yus), the Orthodox code of modesty in dress

yarmulke (YAH-mul-kuh), a skullcap worn by Orthodox men

yeshiva (yeh-SHIV-ah), a Hebrew school

Yeshua (YESH-oo-ah), Jesus

YHWH (not spoken aloud), the letters representing the most holy name for God

Yom Kippur (yom KIP-er), the Day of Atonement, a high holy day celebrated by fasting and the recitation of prayers

Notes

Chapter 5

1. David Dawson, "Why Are We So Indifferent About Our Spiritual Lives?" in *Why Are We Here? Everyday Questions and the Christian Life*, ed. Ronald F. Theimann and William C. Placher (Harrisburg, PA: Trinity Press International, 1998), 20.

Chapter 9

1. Lauren Winner, *Girl Meets God* (New York: Random House, 2002), 163.

About the Author

MARIA POGGI JOHNSON grew up in Scotland and studied at Oxford University and the University of Virginia. She lives with her husband and four children in Northeastern Pennsylvania, and teaches theology at the University of Scranton.